To: Sherrie Lynn
In your search for the
Truth &
The Life

VOLUME TWO

INSIGHT'S BIBLE COMPANION

PRACTICAL HELPS FOR BETTER STUDY

Love — Mom
8/1/00

INSIGHT FOR LIVING

Insight's Bible Companion, volume 2

Copyright © 2000 by Insight for Living

Published by:
    Insight for Living
    Post Office Box 69000
    Anaheim, California 92817-0900
    www.insight.org

ISBN 1-57972-336-5

Unless otherwise identified, all Scripture references are from the New American Standard Bible [NASB], updated edition, copyright © The Lockman Foundation 1960, 1962, 1963, 1968, 1971, 1972, 1973, 1975, 1977, 1995. Used by permission. Also cited is the Holy Bible, New International Version © 1973 1978, 1984 The International Bible Society, used by permission of Zondervan Publishing House.

Cover images: © 2000, Tamara Reynolds/Stone Images

Cover design by Alex Pasieka

Printed in the United States of America

TABLE OF CONTENTS

WELCOME TO THE GALLERY OF SCRIPTURE

There's nothing I enjoy more than a walk down the corridors of Scripture. I'm so glad that in the next pages, we'll be companions during this thoughtful stroll through the hallowed halls of God's inspired Word.

We'll enter through the portico of the Old Testament art galleries where pictures of Noah, Abraham, Moses, Joseph, Isaac, and Daniel hang on the wall. Next, we'll pass through the conservatory of Psalms, where each reed and pipe of God's great organ declares His glory.

Because we recognize Scripture's relevance to everyday life, we'll enter the business office of Proverbs. We'll also venture into the prophets' observatory room, where telescopes of various sizes point to far-off events, all of which focus on the Bright and Morning Star, Who rises above the hills of Judea for our salvation.

Surrounding us on the hills, we can catch a vision for Jesus our Savior's glory from the different perspectives of Matthew, Mark, Luke, and John. Next, we'll visit the nursery where the Holy Spirit raised the infant church. Then we'll peak into the correspondence room, where Paul, Peter, James, and John sit, penning their epistles.

As our visit draws to a close, we'll step into the throne room of Revelation where we catch a vision of the King sitting upon the throne in all His glory.

Around each corner of God's magnificent masterwork, there's a panorama awaiting our exploration. Each of these articles in this *Insight's Bible Companion,* volume 2, written by our very own Insight for Living staff, will provide you with a tour guide's perspective of

God's Word. It's designed to make your Bible study discoveries easier, more practical, and of course, on course with God's plan. We're glad to be travelling companions with you and we look forward to the grand tour through God's Word.

Charles R. Swindoll

VOLUME TWO

INSIGHT'S
BIBLE
COMPANION

PRACTICAL HELPS
FOR
BETTER STUDY

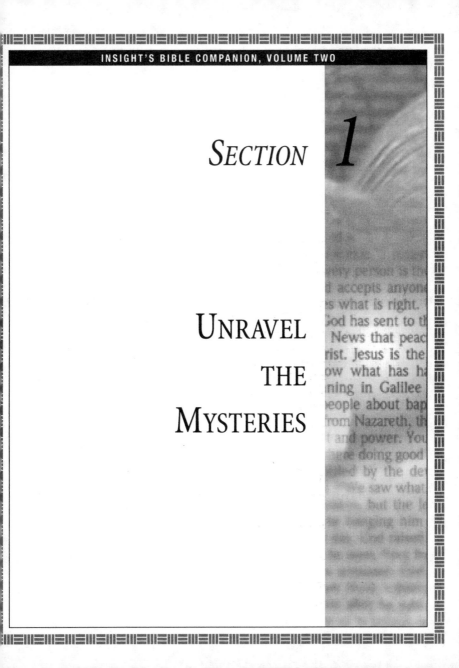

SECTION *1*

UNRAVEL

THE

MYSTERIES

THE FUTURE OF GOD'S PLAN

by Charles R. Swindoll

Let's admit it—the future can be worrisome. It isn't the past that gives us our greatest anxiety. It isn't even the present that disturbs us the most. It's the unseen tomorrow. It's that area in which we really have questions about who is in control. Hindsight invariably has twenty-twenty vision. Looking back, things make sense. But look into tomorrow, and you can't see anything.

More often than not, people not only look to God's Word for what has happened, but also for what is *going* to happen. I have great news for you, my friend! Scripture can be trusted at both ends of God's program. As John Heywood, a sixteenth-century writer of English proverbs, wrote, "All's well that ends well." In God's chronological program, all will end well. We want to know—especially when life is hard or when we agonize over history's unfair twists and turns—that everything is going to turn out okay. We want the assurance that prophecy provides. The God of heaven, Whom we serve and in Whom we believe, is not on the edge of heaven wondering, "What in the world is taking place down there?" or "How did that nation get into that condition?" or "What am I going to do about it?"

If for no other reason, let our discussion of the earth's "end times" affirm to you that our heavenly Father knows precisely what is going to happen. His timepiece runs in precise, perfect order.

Prophecy: A Balanced Approach

Those who study prophecy can easily become tempted toward great imbalance, usually revealed in two areas. The first is predicting dates (common among prophecy fanatics). "The Lord will return in the year . . ." and they fill in the blank. The other extreme that goes along with it is a smug, super-spiritual, I-know-it-all-as-it-relates-to-the-future attitude. You're not going to find either side of that pendulum-swing in this or any other prophetic study from Insight for Living.

When I'm gone, if I'm long since forgotten for most everything else, I hope I will be remembered for one thing: balance. My one great desire before God is to be a balanced man, a balanced preacher, and a balanced expositor—not always in the Old Testament, but not always in the New Testament. Not always on the subject of prophecy, but not always ignoring prophecy. Not always on some profound part of the spiritual life, and yet not always overlooking it, either. I want to apply that same balance to our study of God's future events. As one of my mentors used to say, "we've been given this prophetic Word not just to satisfy idle curiosity, but also to change lives."

A Great Time to Live

In the panorama of this world's timeline, we live in the church age. God gave birth to the church in Acts 2. We have the joy and the privilege of living in a time in which the Spirit of God universally indwells all of His children, His Word is open and understood, and evangelism sweeps through many parts of the land. It's a marvelous era in which to live—so different from the days of the Law with sacrifices and a rigid lifestyle. The freedom of grace, the beauty of worship, and so many technical capabilities that we just take for granted—we experience all of that in the church age.

This time stands out from other times in history for three distinct reasons: first of all, there is no longer a distinction between Jew or Gentile. The same is true whether you come to know Christ as a proud Jew, or as a pagan Gentile. You still come into the family of God. This was never true prior to Acts 2, back in the days of the Law.

Second, we do not know how long the age in which we now live will last. Scripture reveals no exit date, regardless of what anyone may tell you.

Third, this era will end with Christ's return for His bride, the church. This is often called the Rapture.

The Next Event: the Rapture

I'm absolutely convinced we are in the very last days of the church. This church age in which we find ourselves will end with the rapture of the church.

For your own perusal in days to come, let me give you some Scriptures which describe these "last days" of the church. Read each one slowly, carefully: 1 Corinthians 15:50–58; John 14:1–3; and 1 Thessalonians 4:13–18. Just to throw you students of prophecy a curve, add Revelation 3:10, which so clearly describes why I'm placing the Rapture where I am in Scripture. Here, the church is promised they will be taken out from (literally, 'out from among') that time of great testing that will sweep the whole world. It's a unique promise that teaches the Rapture and its place in God's prophetic plan.

Now, let me give you a couple of distinctions of the Rapture. First, all living and dead believers (the key word is *believers*) will be removed from planet earth. The second distinction is rather obvious: only unbelievers will be left on the earth. Those of us who are living at the time of the Rapture will be literally caught up to be with Christ when He returns for us.

As I see it, the Rapture is the next major event in God's future program. I anticipate it every day. The anticipation comes to me more often when I'm under great testing than when things are going well.

3

It's a great hope, a great comfort, and a great encouragement. I've hung on to that song: "O Lord Jesus, how long, how long / 'Til we shout the glad song / Christ returneth! Hallelujah!   . . ."

Listen to the words of Paul:

> But we do not want you to be uninformed, brethren, about those who are asleep, so that you will not grieve, even as do the rest who have no hope. For if we believe that Jesus died and rose again, even so God will bring with Him those who have fallen asleep in Jesus. For this we say to you by the word of the Lord, that we who are alive and remain until the coming of the Lord, will not precede those who have fallen asleep. (1 Thess. 4:13–15)

He then gives the order of events:

> For the Lord Himself will descend from heaven with a shout, with the voice of the archangel, and with the trumpet of God, and the dead in Christ will rise first. Then we who are alive and remain will be caught up together with them in the clouds to meet the Lord in the air, and so we shall always be with the Lord. (vv. 16–18)

Brothers and sisters in the church age, that's hope! Living and dead will be changed *instantly* and *permanently* as we're taken to be with the Lord *eternally*. Do you know what else it spells? It spells disaster. Now why? Because that leaves this old earth in chaotic condition. With all believers taken away, can you imagine the turmoil, the confusion in homes and businesses, and half-full churches?

Some of you reading this, quite frankly, will be left because, up to this point in your life, you've never come to know Jesus Christ. You may be counting on church membership or a good moral background, or being around Christians to get you into heaven. You've not yet humbled your heart before God and expressed a prayer like this: "I'm a sinner. I need hope. I need help. I need forgiveness. I need Your love. I need Your grace. Today—right this moment—I take Jesus as my Savior . . . my Master . . . my own Redeemer."

I plead with you, if you learn nothing else from prophecy, learn the importance of being ready for His coming. The best way to be ready is to be in Christ. Ready or not, He's coming! He is coming soon! And that coming could be at *anytime,* day or night. There is every evidence on the surface of Scripture, as well as in our times, that His presence draws near. He could even come today before the clock strikes midnight. (Wouldn't that be great?)

Child of God, your future is in God's hands. All the world's future events are in His hands. His sovereign arrangement of those future events replaces fear with peace. He has a handle on the order in which they will transpire. As the Bible teaches, "Our times are in His hands." One of the greatest verses I've ever learned is:

> All the inhabitants of the earth are as nothing, but
> He does according to His will in the host of heaven
> and among the inhabitants of the earth; and no one
> can stay His hand or say unto Him, "What have you
> done?" (Dan. 4:35)

Isn't that a magnificent statement! When we wonder, "God, what are You doing?" Daniel says, "Even when you can't understand it, His plan is unfolding. Count on it. He knows what He's about."

Since God knows what He's about, you and I can trust Him with tomorrow. So? So . . . trust Him!

REVELATION: JOURNEY TO THE *REAL* NEW MILLENNIUM

by Larry Sittig

How we wish we could stretch up on tiptoes, squint hard, and peer off into the distance to see . . . the future. What will be on the test tomorrow? Whom will I marry? Which stocks will go up in value? What tragedies will threaten my family? We want to know the future so we can feel less fearful and more confident. We want to know how to prepare today for what's coming tomorrow.

The desire to see into the future, even if the future is frightening as can be, became a big part of the closing years, months, and days of the second Christian millennium. Many Christians, and unbelievers too, with reasons ranging from the serious to the absurd, were afraid that the calendar's flip from 1999 to 2000 would bring on cataclysmic, and even apocalyptic, events. Though the ominous deadline passed without major problems, we all learned again how we long to peek around those dark corners of life to know what awaits us.

In the Scriptures, God seemed to let His people have the clearest views into the future at the times when their present perspective was the most distressing. When the exile to Babylon threatened to extinguish Israel's flame, God sent prophets like Isaiah, Ezekiel, and Daniel to show that Israel would be restored to blessing, and that the glorious kingdom of God would one day overwhelm the corrupt kingdoms of humanity. Then, when the crushing weight of Roman persecution fell upon first-century Christians, God opened up a window of hope, a door to the future, to an aging apostle exiled on an island in the Aegean Sea.

The book of Revelation tells us the story of the Apostle John's inspired vision. He was exposed to sights, sounds, and multiplied other sensations that went well beyond his capacity to comprehend, much less explain. Through all that he experienced, John was assured—and assures us—that the Lamb of God will reign as King over the entire world, with His faithful servants by His side.

Why did God give us this "revelation?" John is clear about that. It is so that we can know the future—"what must soon take place" (Rev. 1:1).[1] But why would God want us to know the future? Certainly it is not to satisfy idle curiosity. As we study the prophecy, we discover a number of reasons for the Revelation:

- ✔ To open our spiritual eyes to more of reality than meets the physical eye

- ✔ To give us confidence in God's purposeful work when everything seems chaotic

- ✔ To help us conquer our fears of suffering and persecution

- ✔ To teach us to worship the Lord Jesus, along with the Father, as the Lord of history and of our own lives

- ✔ To nurture our aversion to evil and our devotion to good—our obedience to Him Who alone is good

---

1. "The word 'soon' (*en tachei*; see 2:16; 22:7, 12, 20) means that the action will be sudden when it comes, not necessarily that it will occur immediately. Once the end-time events begin, they will occur in rapid succession ([see] Luke 18:8; Acts 12:7; 22:18; 25:4; Rom. 16:20)." From John F. Walvoord, *The Bible Knowledge Commentary,* New Testament edition (Wheaton, Ill.: Scripture Press Publications, Victor Books, 1983), p. 928.

8

So what did John see? The answers to that question have been diverse and often contradictory:

✔ Some say that John is describing, in symbolic terms, dramatic events that were taking place in his own lifetime, such as the destruction of Jerusalem and the Roman Emperor's persecution of early Christians. Theologians call this the *preterist view.*

✔ Others say John's vision is a review of all the ages since Christ's first coming, approaching a climax in His imminent return in glory. It's called the *historicist view.*

✔ Many see the Revelation as a collection of images that symbolically depict the eternal struggle between good and evil, in which God will triumph. This is the *idealist view.*

✔ Some understand John's vision to represent the climactic final events of history, in which God will judge Satan and rebellious humanity and Christ will establish His promised Kingdom. This is known as the *futurist view.*[2]

So how do we decide which of these views faithfully represents God's intent in giving us the book of Revelation? Whenever we examine a message that's hard to understand, especially one that is as full of symbolism as Revelation is, we try to draw out its meaning using

---

2. One of the major issues in the discussion of prophecy is the interpretation of Revelation 20:1–6, which speaks of Christ imprisoning Satan and reigning for a thousand years. The three main options are: *amillennialism*, which understands the figure of a thousand years to be symbolic, and sees Christ reigning now and forever in heaven and in believers; *postmillennialism*, which sees Christ coming to gradually extend His rule over the world through the preaching of the gospel and the growth of righteousness; and *premillennialism*, the view that Christ will literally fulfill the promise to come and to reign. The proponents of the first two views may hold any of the four forms of interpretation detailed above. Premillennialism, because of its commitment to normal or literal interpretation, is consistently committed to the futurist interpretation of Revelation.

any interpretive clues we can bring to the text. It's important that we come to the text with the right set of clues. The futurist interpretation of this book brings its interpretive clues to Revelation from the best source: from the Bible itself, especially those portions of the Bible that are of the same type, the other prophetic and apocalyptic books. When John was moved by the Holy Spirit to paint us a word picture of the vision he had been given, he chose for his palette the brushes and colors he inherited from Daniel, from Ezekiel, from other prophets, and from the Lord Jesus Himself. To best interpret John's inspired writing, we need to draw from the same sources.[3]

With this interpretive framework in place, we can follow the simple outline for Revelation that is written out for us in chapter 1, verse 19. The Lord Jesus told John to write down:

✔ "What you have seen . . ." (chap. 1): The vision of the resurrected, glorified Savior.

✔ "What is now . . ." (chaps. 2–3): The messages to the churches.

✔ "And what will take place later" (chaps. 4–22): The calling of the Church into the throne room of God (4–5); the judgments and grace of God in the period of Great Tribulation (6–18); Christ's return to reign for a thousand years, judging sinners, and vanquishing evil (19–20); and the inauguration of the new heavens and new earth (21–22).

---

3. For example, "Many of the symbols in Daniel's visions reappear in John's, such as the lion, bear, leopard, and beast (compare Dan. 7 and Rev. 13). The catastrophic time in Revelation 6–18 closely aligns with Daniel's seventieth week (Dan. 9:27) and Jesus' 'great tribulation' (Matt. 24:15–27). Also, the Second Coming in Revelation 1:17 and 19:11–21 parallels Daniel 7:11–14, 21–27 and Matthew 24:29–31." Taken from the study guide *God's Masterwork: A Concerto in Sixty-Six Movements, Volume 5,* coauthored by Gary Matlack and Bryce Klabunde, from the Bible-teaching ministry of Charles R. Swindoll (Anaheim, Calif.: Insight for Living, 1998), p. 126.

These principles will help us stay on the right track when we read the book of Revelation:

1. **Major on the majors.** Some things are crystal clear. The main outline is strong and straight. Don't get mired in the nonessentials.

2. **Scripture interprets Scripture more authoritatively than we interpret Scripture.** The best interpretive keys to John's message and his symbolism are the prophetic books of the Old Testament. He's especially linked to the Old Testament apocalypse of Daniel. There are also some important clues in Christ's apocalyptic address in Matthew 24.

3. **If the normal sense makes good sense, seek no other sense.**

4. **Don't use symbols to engage in unwarranted speculation.** A symbol represents an essential trait of the person or thing it represents. Our task is to draw out those essential points of comparison, not to make the comparison work from every possible angle.

5. **Take it to heart.** Blessing is promised to the person who hears and heeds the words of this prophecy (Rev. 1:3; 22:7). We can't change the course of God's prophetic plans. So let's focus our attention on learning what He teaches, desiring what He desires, being in awe of His majesty, and loving and knowing Him.

Only the Lamb of God is worthy (chap. 5) to take the reins of history and bring about the Father's glorious purposes in this millennium, the *real* millennium, and throughout eternity. No matter when or how the Apocalypse predicted in John's prophecy is fulfilled, those of us who are in Christ can face the future with confidence.

Bibliography

Benware, Paul N. *Understanding End Times Prophecy: A Comprehensive Approach.* Chicago, Ill.: Moody Press, 1995.

Dyer, Charles H. *World News and Bible Prophecy.* Wheaton, Ill.: Tyndale House Publishers, 1993.

Swindoll, Charles R., John F. Walvoord, J. Dwight Pentecost, and others. *The Road to Armageddon.* Nashville, Tenn.: Word Publishing, 1999.

Walvoord, John F. "Revelation." *The Bible Knowledge Commentary,* New Testament edition. John F. Walvoord and Roy B. Zuck, eds. Wheaton, Ill.: Scripture Press Publications, Victor Books, 1983.

PROPHETS AND APOCALYPSE: TRUTH ON A COLLISION COURSE

by Larry Sittig

President Abraham Lincoln liked to speak of a man who, when he was tarred and feathered and ridden out of town on a rail, wryly—and painfully—remarked, "If it wasn't for the honor of the thing, I'd rather walk." The now universally admired American president was, during his life, sometimes severely attacked by his critics. President Lincoln's words offer us a glimpse, through his dry wit, into the inner pain of many who stand in the public spotlight. The prophets of the Old Testament often must have felt the same kind of distress. Sure, they were privileged to stand before kings and multitudes to proclaim the Word of the Lord. But what they received in return was, more often than not, harsh rejection and intense suffering.

These suffering servants of God faithfully delivered their divine messages while absorbing hateful opposition and even violence (see Jesus' words in Luke 11:47–51) . Because of their faithfulness, they serve as models for believers of all generations. We too are called to speak the Word of God in a context where many are moving away from obedience to it, especially many of those who enjoy power and influence. The prophets are our older brothers and sisters, and our examples in the faith.

If we will wade into their sometimes tangled historical and cultural context to get to know the biblical prophets, we'll find ourselves transfixed and transformed by their vision. Through the inspired messages they left as their legacies, the prophets unveil to us the strong emotions and unwavering intentions of God. They challenge each one of us to heart-wrenching repentance and odds-defying hopefulness. They inspire us to passionate faithfulness and evil-vanquishing courage.

Though earlier patriarchs functioned as God's spokesmen, the office of prophet was first recognized when Moses instructed the people to give heed to each one who, like him, would deliver God's special revelation to them (Deut. 18:14–22). On the day of Pentecost, Peter announced that the One of whom Moses spoke had come, uniquely and finally, in the person of our Lord Jesus Christ (Acts 3:22–23). The prophets, unlike kings and priests, were not born into their office. These men and women (see Exod. 15:20; Judg. 4:4) were called, sometimes against their wills, when God revealed Himself to them and declared His intention to use them as His mouthpiece (see Jer. 1:4–10; 20:14–18; Amos 7:14; and Jon. 1:1–3, as well as Isa. 6 and Ezek. 2). He also must have strengthened the resolve of those He called (as in Ezek. 3:8–9), because true prophets stood like steer in a blizzard, upholding the truth before people who scorned the message and attacked the messenger.

Many of the earlier prophets served in the court of the kings of Judah and Israel, advising them and, as was often necessary, confronting them. For instance, it was the prophet Nathan who piercingly accused King David of his sins of adultery, murder, and the abuse of power (2 Sam. 12:1–14). As time went by, other prophets began to address their messages to the whole nation. They wrote down their prophecies to denounce the unfaithfulness of the people and to warn of coming judgment. Their words are recorded, as the Holy Spirit inspired them to write, in the five books of the major prophets (Isaiah through Daniel, called "major" simply because the books are longer) and the twelve books of the minor prophets (Hosea through Malachi).

It's helpful to identify the prophets of the Old Testament by their relationships to the history of God's people and by the messages they proclaimed. Here are some examples:

History	Prophet	Message
Founding of the nation of Israel	Moses	"'A kingdom of priests and a holy nation'" (Exod. 19:6).
Period of the judges	Deborah	"'The honor . . . to a woman'" (Judg. 4:9).
	Samuel	"'The evil of asking for a king'" (1 Sam. 12:19).
To the kings of the united monarchy period	Nathan	"'You are the man!'" (2 Sam. 12:7).
After Judah and Israel divided	Hosea	"'Let [Israel] put away her harlotry . . .'" (Hos. 2:2).
	Obadiah	"'The day of the Lord draws near on all the nations'" (Obad. 15).
	Jonah	"'I knew that you are a gracious and compassionate God'" (Jon. 4:2).
Judah after Israel fell	Amos	"Seek Me that you may live" (Amos 5:4).
	Isaiah	"By His knowledge the Righteous One, My Servant, will justify the many, as He will bear their iniquities" (Isa. 53:11).
	Jeremiah	"I . . . weep day and night for the slain of . . . my people!" (Jer. 9:1).
	Joel	"'I will make up to you for the years that the swarming locust has eaten'" (Joel 2:25).
Judah's exile in Babylon	Ezekiel	"'I will give you a new heart and put a new spirit within you'" (Ezek. 36:26).
	Daniel	"His kingdom is an everlasting kingdom" (Dan. 4:3).
After the return to Palestine	Haggai	"'I will fill this house with glory'" (Hag. 2:7).
	Zechariah	"Your king is coming to you" (Zech. 9:9).

While they most frequently issued denunciations and warnings, the prophets declared as well that God would triumph in history, fulfilling His promises to the faithful remnant of His people. Over a prolonged period of moral decline and calamitous judgment, the armies of Assyria, and then Babylon, reduced God's chosen people to a ragged band of exiles and subservient peasants. Even in those circumstances, through the apocalyptic visions of the prophets, God sustained in His people the hope that all would be turned around for the good.

Apocalypse: The Drama of Hope

Apocalypse is a form of literature well-suited for people who live in a world where all appearances point to God's absence or powerlessness. Some of the prophets were swept above the earthly sphere and given visions of more reality than the naked eye could see and common words could describe. Because of this, apocalyptic literature necessarily involves large measures of symbolism and mystery. But a threefold message comes through with force and brilliance.

First, God is in control of every detail of history (read Dan. 4:34–35; Rev. 5:5). Second, He will conquer evil and rule through His restored covenant people (Dan. 7:13–18; Rev. 19:11–20:6). Third, this calls for humble repentance, faithful obedience, and hopeful perseverance from those who are called by His name (Ezek. 36:24–38; Matt. 24:42–51; Rev. 2–3).

In the Old Testament, the great apocalyptic visions are recorded for us in Isaiah 24–27; Daniel 7–12; Ezekiel; Obadiah; and Joel.[1] In

---

1. Because of the powerful, miraculous nature of the Old Testament prophetic apocalypses, especially Daniel's vision of successive historic kingdoms, a number of imitation apocalypses were written in the Jewish community in the two centuries before Christ and during the first Christian century. Scholars who do not recognize the unique inspiration of the books of the Bible group the biblical apocalyptic visions with them. But these other writings are clearly human reproductions that only highlight the distinct quality of the originals. See, for example, George Eldon Ladd, "Apocalyptic Literature," in *The International Standard Bible Encyclopedia,* gen. ed. Geoffrey W. Bromiley (Grand Rapids, Mich.: William B. Eerdmans Publishing Co., 1979), vol. 1, pp. 151–161.

the New Testament, apocalyptic literature is given for our instruction and encouragement in Matthew 24; Mark 13; and of course, in the book of Revelation.

The prophets of the Old Testament all looked forward to the coming of the promised King (Luke 24:27; Acts 3:24). In the New Testament, prophets were sent to guide the Church in its understanding of the first coming of the Lord Jesus, and in its anticipation of His return (1 Cor. 12:28, Eph. 2:19–20). They spoke revealed truth to the church until the prophetic Scriptures were inspired by the Holy Spirit to give a certain word to all of humanity. Every time we open up our Bibles, we come face-to-face with an inspired prophet (see 2 Pet. 1:19–21)

Unfortunately, few Christians accept the challenge to dig deeply into the prophetic books of the Bible. We may feel like the Israelite king who said he hated the prophet Micaiah because he never had anything good to say (1 Kings 22:8). And, we may feel entirely intimidated by the strange images and symbols of the prophetic visions. But the Bible promises a rich reward to those who dig deep into the gem-laden mines of prophetic Scripture (Prov. 2; Rev. 1:3). A richer, deeper view of our sovereign God, faith to sustain us in dark, turbulent times, courage to speak God's Word where it must be heard, and the purifying power of a vision of the glorified Christ—these are the honors heaped on those who will come alongside the prophets—even if we get a bit too close at times to their tar and feathers.

Bibliography

Feinberg, Charles L. *The Minor Prophets.* Chicago, Ill.: Moody Press, 1976.

Merrill, Eugene H. *Kingdom of Priests: A History of Old Testament Israel.* Grand Rapids, Mich.: Baker Book House, 1987.

God's Masterwork: A Concerto in Sixty-Six Movements, Volume 2: Ezra through Daniel and *Volume 3: Hosea through Malachi.* Coauthored by Gary Matlack, from the Bible-teaching ministry of Charles R. Swindoll. Anaheim, Calif.: Insight for Living, 1997.

Wood, Leon J. *The Prophets of Israel.* Grand Rapids, Mich.: Baker Book House, 1979.

CLUES TO UNDERSTANDING JESUS' PARABLES

by Bryce Klabunde

Jesus' parables have sparked imaginations and inspired hearts for almost two thousand years. A father embraces his repentant prodigal son. A kind-hearted Samaritan treats the wounds of a fallen stranger. A shepherd risks his life to rescue a single lost lamb. These brief yet powerful stories have motivated countless acts of grace and love. Indeed, the truths in Jesus' parables have shaped the conscience of entire societies and, in many ways, changed the course of humankind.

Yet Jesus' parables often are as puzzling as they are powerful. What is the significance of pouring new wine into old wineskins? How can yeast in dough explain the kingdom of heaven? And how does a fruitless fig tree relate to Jesus' message of repentance?

We need some guiding concepts to help us solve these parable mysteries. Here are four clues that can assist you in your study.

Clue 1: The Audience

The first clue to unlocking the meaning of a parable is Jesus' original audience. He often addressed His parables to large crowds, which, depending on the setting, would have been characterized by specific groups of people. If He was preaching in the countryside, His audience would have been landowners, foremen, and farmers. If He was addressing a city crowd, they would have been merchants and craftsman. And if He was near the sea, they would have been fishermen and boat builders.

Sometimes Jesus addressed His parable to a small group of disciples or to individuals—such as a lawyer or a proud Pharisee or a prostitute weeping at His feet.

Understanding the audience provides important clues to understanding the purpose and message of the parable. A few questions to consider as you reflect on the audience might be these:

✔ What makes this parable particularly suited to this audience?

✔ How would this audience react, positively or negatively, to the various elements in the parable?

✔ What might the audience be thinking or feeling as they listen to the parable?

Clue 2: The Points of Reference

Points of reference are the elements in the parable with which the audience immediately identifies. In their book, *How to Read the Bible for All Its Worth,* Gordon Fee and Douglas Stuart explain points of reference as "those parts of the story that draw the hearer into it."[1] They are the literary "carrots" that lead the listener out of his or her mistaken way of thinking to a new, more challenging perspective.

For example, the prophet Nathan used points of reference to convict David of his secret sin with Bathsheba. In His parable, a poor man owns a single lamb that he loves dearly. David, who was a shepherd as a boy, immediately identifies with the poor man's affection for his sheep. This point of reference draws David into the story and causes him to react in anger when a rich man steals the poor man's lamb and slaughters it for a feast. When Nathan compares David to the heartless rich man, David finally feels the full weight of guilt for his sin.

---

1. Gordon D. Fee and Douglas Stuart, *How to Read the Bible for All Its Worth* (Grand Rapids, Mich.: Zondervan Publishing House, Academie Books, 1982), p. 128.

Can you identify the points of reference in Jesus' parables? Use your knowledge of the audience to help you locate them.

✔ Audience: farmers who barely scratch out a living on the rocky hillsides of Judea. What are the points of reference in The Sower and the Soils (Luke 8:5–15)? For example, the farmers' disappointment over the seed that never took root.

✔ Audience: sinners and outcasts who are shunned by the religious elite. What are the points of reference in The Prodigal Son (Luke 15:11–32)? For example, the sinners' identification with the son's pursuit of pleasure.

✔ Audience: social climbers who elbow for positions of honor at a luncheon. What are the points of reference in The Great Banquet (Luke 14:15–24)? For example, the social significance of sitting in the place of honor.

Clue 3: The Plot Twist

The third clue to the meaning of the parable is the plot twist, the turn of events that surprises—often, stuns—the audience. In some cases, the plot twist delivers a blow of conviction. "You are the man!" Nathan announces to David, as he jabs the message of the parable into the king's gut.

In other cases, the plot twist delivers a surprising and hopeful ray of light that reveals a way out of their darkness. In The Prodigal Son, for example, the father surprises the son by slipping his own ring on his son's finger—giving hope to all prodigals who long to come home to their heavenly Father. In The Workers in the Vineyard, the surprise is the landowner paying the late workers the same wage as those who labored all day. In The Great Banquet, it's the king inviting the lame and the poor to enjoy the feast his rich guests ignored.

Identifying the plot twist is a crucial clue in solving the mystery of the parable. But there's one more clue to investigate, and this one is perhaps the most difficult.

Clue 4: The Meaning of the Parts

Unlike in typical stories, the characters and objects in parables often represent something larger than the story itself. In The Sower and the Soils, the seed represents the message of the kingdom, and the soils represent the various conditions of people's hearts when they hear the message. Many of the other parts are symbolic too. For instance, the birds represent the Evil One; the thorns, the worries of this life; and the crop, the fruit of faith. Jesus Himself interprets these parts for us, so we can be certain of their identity.

In parables that Jesus doesn't interpret, the identity of the elements is not as clear, and we should take care not to let our interpretations run wild. Parables are not allegories, in which each part represents something completely foreign to the context. Augustine allegorized The Good Samaritan, interpreting the wounded man as Adam, the thieves as demons, the oil as the comfort of hope, the inn as the church, and so on.[2] This approach destroys the beauty and simplicity of the parable and distorts the message.

When attempting to interpret the parts of a parable, let the context guide the meaning. Keep in mind this rule of thumb: the most obvious meaning is the most likely meaning. And remember, it isn't necessary to identify every grain of sand in a parable.

The Mystery Solved

You might think of these four clues as pieces of a puzzle that join together to reveal a complete picture. And when we see the full picture of a parable, we can more easily decipher its message. Parables

---

2. Fee and Stuart, *How to Read the Bible for All Its Worth*, p. 124

usually only have one message, and you should be able to summarize that message in a sentence or two. The Good Samaritan's message, for example, is this: "We can love our neighbors by caring for the hurting people around us."

One last thought. When studying a parable, be careful of stripping its message and leaving the story behind. In many ways, the message and the story can't be separated, for the story is the message. Remember, parables are designed not merely to inform us but to inspire us. The plot, the emotional plea, the surprise ending, the symbolic elements—all these components of a good story help bring the truth to life. And once it is alive, the truth just might change our world.

BIBLICAL ARCHAEOLOGY: CONFIRMING THE HISTORICAL ACCURACY OF SCRIPTURE

by Mike Balsbaugh

The Christian faith finds its roots in history. The Bible tells the story of real people who lived commonplace lives. These people worked hard to earn their living and raise their children. They went shopping, sang their favorite songs, and fought wars with nations and diseases. They were not mythical, superhuman characters—they were folks like us.

Moses got sweaty and tired as he climbed Mount Sinai to receive the Ten Commandments. John baptized people in a river that left them wet, chilly, and muddy as they returned to the shore. The woman at the well carried a clay pot that a craftsman had spent several hours making. David played a harp that required regular tuning. Jesus fed more than five thousand people who had left their chores behind to listen to Him.

Why are these observations important? Because if its characters and events are fictitious, the Bible is merely another inspirational book for our enjoyment. But if the events in Scripture happened in a real place with actual people at a particular point in time, then we had better sit up and pay close attention. If the Bible gives us a historically accurate record, we must respond to its claims. We must obey its truths and bow to its God.

No wonder, then, the historical accuracy of the Bible has been so fiercely attacked. Enemies of the Scriptures know that if they can prove the Bible as not historically credible, then its message becomes utterly irrelevant.

Thankfully, archaeologists have served us well. For the past two hundred years, they have been digging up treasures from biblical times. And what they have uncovered has repeatedly verified the testimony of Scripture, showing that what the Bible said happened *really* happened. The following list of treasures gives us a sampling of their discoveries.

✔ **The Dead Sea Scrolls:** These scrolls, preserved in caves overlooking the Dead Sea, contain hundreds of manuscripts of the Scriptures and other writings. They include a complete copy of the book of Isaiah dating from about 100 B.C. With the exception of Esther, every Old Testament book is represented. This is an important discovery because these old copies of the Scriptures are nearly identical to Hebrew manuscripts copied a thousand years later. This affirms the accuracy of the Bible we read today by showing how carefully the Scriptures have been copied over time.[1]

✔ **The Israel Stele:** This Egyptian granite slab commemorates several of Pharaoh Meneptah's military victories, including his defeat of Israel. A date of about 1220 B.C. makes this the earliest extra-biblical reference to the nation of Israel. It identifies the Hebrews living in the land of Palestine during the period of the Judges. This find helps confirm the biblical date of the Exodus, a date critics have long challenged.[2]

---

1. E. M. Blaiklock and R. K. Harrison, gen. ed., *The New International Dictionary of Biblical Archaeology* (Grand Rapids, Mich.: Zondervan Publishing House, 1983), pp. 154–57.

2. Blaiklock and Harrison, *The New International Dictionary of Biblical Archaeology,* pp. 254–255.

✔ **The inscriptions in the great temple of Karnak in Egypt:**
These record Pharaoh Shishak's defeat of Jerusalem. This event,
recorded in 1 Kings 14, took place during the reign of Rehoboam,
David's grandson.[3]

✔ **Personal seals:** In the past twenty-five years, archaeologists digging in Jerusalem have discovered a number of ancient clay
stamps used to seal and authenticate important documents.
Several of them bore the names of people in the Bible. The most
exciting were two seals belonging to Baruch, son of Neriah,
Jeremiah's personal scribe (Jer. 32; 36; 43; 45). One of the seals
has his fingerprint pressed into the clay! Five other biblical per-
sonalities are represented in the seals as well. They are Azaliah
(2 Kings 22:3), Hilkiah (Jer. 29:3), Gemariah (Jer. 36:10),
Jerahmeel (Jer. 36:26), and Seraiah (Jer. 51:59).[4]

✔ **The Moabite Stone:** This nineteenth-century discovery describes
Israel's rule over Moab during the reign of King Ahab and the
subsequent Moabite rebellion against Israel during the reign of
King Joram. This extrabiblical record affirms the events recorded
in 2 Kings 3:4–27.[5]

✔ **The royal chronicles of Sargon II:** These records of the
Assyrian king, discovered in 1843, tell of the fall of Samaria just
as it is recorded in 2 Kings 17 and 18.[6]

3. Joseph P. Free, *Archaeology and Bible History,* rev. and exp. Howard F. Vos (Grand Rapids,
Mich.: Zondervan Publishing House, 1992), p. 154.

4. Hershel Shanks, *Jerusalem: An Archaeological Biography* (New York, N.Y.: Random House,
1995), pp. 107–109.

5. Free, *Archaeology and Bible History*, pp. 160–61.

6. Free, *Archaeology and Bible History*, pp. 169–70.

✔ **The Taylor Cylinder:** Discovered in Nineveh in 1830, this Assyrian artifact tells of King Sennacherib's war with Judah, and his failure to conquer Jerusalem (see 2 Kings 18–19). While Sennacherib boasts of conquering many Judean cities, he simply says that he shut Hezekiah up in Jerusalem like a caged bird. Apparently, this was Sennacherib's "good spin" on failing to take Jerusalem. His account confirms that God did indeed deliver Jerusalem from destruction.[7]

✔ **The annals of Esarhaddon:** Esarhaddon, Sennacherib's son, recorded his father's untimely death at the hands of Esarhaddon's two brothers (see 2 Kings 19:37).[8]

✔ **Historical documents verifying the existence of Jesus:** These establish Christ as a real, living person—something that is still challenged today. Tacitus, a Roman historian writing around A.D. 100, records that Christ was executed at the hands of the Pontius Pilate in the reign of Tiberius. Pliny the Younger, a governor in Asia Minor (modern Turkey), wrote to Emperor Trajan in A.D. 111 for advice on dealing with Christians, whose allegiance was "to Christ, their founder." Another Roman writer, Lucian of Samosata (circa A.D. 125–190), writes about Christ—the originator of Christianity—and His crucifixion in Palestine. In addition to these writers, the Jewish historian Flavius Josephus and many early church fathers gave testimony to the historicity of Jesus.[9]

✔ **The Pilate inscription:** Discovered in Caesarea in 1961, clear reference is made to Pontius Pilate. Before this find, there was no

---

7. Free, *Archaeology and Bible History,* pp. 179–80.

8. Free, *Archaeology and Bible History*, p. 180.

9. Free, *Archaeology and Bible History,* p. 243–244.

direct archaeological evidence for Pilate's existence, leading some critics to question the accuracy of the Bible's reference to him.[10]

These are just a few examples of the many archaeological discoveries that verify the historical claims of the Bible. In addition to the finds that point to a specific event or person in Scripture, archaeology supports and verifies many customs and cultural traditions described in the Bible.

Is our faith based on the proofs of archaeology? No. But as archaeology continually confirms the biblical record, it strengthens our confidence in the Scriptures and enhances our credibility with anyone who asks us to "give the reason for the hope that we have" (1 Pet. 3:15).

Bibliography

Blaiklock, E. M. and R. K. Harrison, general editors. *The New International Dictionary of Biblical Archaeology.* Grand Rapids, Mich.: Zondervan Publishing House, 1983.

Free, Joseph P., revised and expanded by Howard F. Vos. *Archaeology and Bible History.* Grand Rapids, Mich.: Zondervan Publishing House, 1992.

Shanks, Hershel. *Jerusalem: An Archaeological Biography.* New York, N.Y.: Random House, 1995.

10. Free, *Archaeology and Bible History,* pp. 238–239.

THE TOPOGRAPHY OF ISRAEL: WHY THE LAY OF THE LAND MATTERS

by Mike Balsbaugh

As any visitor to Israel can tell you, the Palestine region is a harsh land with semi-arid climate and tiring terrain. Though fertile areas dot the landscape, much of Israel's history occurred in the hills, where the rocky soil made for an exhausting lifestyle. Certainly you can find beauty in the Holy Land, but you may also question if God could have chosen a more favorable location for the Promised Land—like Switzerland or France.

Of course, God knew exactly what He was doing when He led Abraham to Canaan. The land of the Bible, commonly known as Palestine, creates the perfect setting for the unfolding of God's story of redemption. Read on to discover four reasons why.

Strategic Location

In the ancient world, civilization developed along the "Fertile Crescent." This term defines a section of the world that begins with Egypt in the south. It runs through Palestine and Syria, arches to the east, and finally encompasses the valleys along the Tigris and Euphrates Rivers in modern-day Iraq.

Because of the ominous desert to the east and the Mediterranean Sea to the north and west, the logical travel route between the two ends of the Fertile Crescent went right through Palestine. This was true for both military and commercial ventures. If you were an Egyptian Pharaoh and had a bone to pick with Babylon, you marched through Palestine. If you were an Assyrian businessman and wanted to trade with an Egyptian craftsman, your caravan would travel through Palestine. Palestine wasn't that important by itself, but its placement at the crossroads between the ancient world's major powers made it the thoroughfare of the Fertile Crescent.

God brought Abraham and his descendants to this land bridge, this thoroughfare. From the beginning, God planned to bless all peoples through Abraham's descendants (Gen. 12:1–3). Living on the main highway of the ancient world put Israel in the best possible place to influence the world for the Lord by being a witness to the nations.

Unfortunately, Israel didn't always live up to her calling. But God's purposes are never thwarted. Jesus, the Light of the World, ministered in the middle of this same land bridge (see Isa. 9:1–3). And after His resurrection and ascension, the church expanded from Israel right along the roads that linked the entire known world. God's calling of Abraham to Palestine two thousand years before Christ illustrates His eternal passion to spread the Good News to the whole world.

Protective Topography

Palestine provided the ideal location for God's plan of redemption because the topography protected the Hebrew nation. Being the smaller kid on the block, Israel was always at a disadvantage, dwarfed by heavy hitters like Egypt, Assyria, and Babylon. But the same hills that made their lives exhausting also protected them. Stationed in the hilly terrain, the Israelites had the advantage. The hills and mountains nullified the speed of chariots, provided shelter, made surprise enemy attacks impractical, and allowed for easier enemy ambushes. If Palestine were a flat plain, Israel's survival would have been much more difficult.

This protective topography became a picture of God's care for

Israel in various passages of Scripture:

> Those who trust in the Lord
> Are like Mount Zion,
>> which cannot be moved but abides forever.
> As the mountains surround Jerusalem,
> So the Lord surrounds His people
> From this time forth and forever. (Ps. 125:1–2)

Dependence-Teaching Land

A third reason Palestine provided the ideal location for God's plan of redemption is that the topography of the land encouraged dependence on God. Much of Israel received meager and unpredictable rainfall. The steep terrain and rocky soil limited much farming. Hills made traveling tiresome. The people of Israel knew they weren't self-sufficient; they needed God. James Monson said of Palestine:

> Natural routes are constricted by uplifted limestone hills, deeply eroded canyons and sharp geological faults. . . .
> . . . This land served as God's *testing ground of faith.* It was here, in this land where both personal and national existence were threatened, that Israel's leaders and people were called upon to learn the true meaning of security and well-being, of trust in the Lord their God.[1]

The Desert Regions

Finally, the land of Palestine sets the perfect stage for God's redemptive plan because of its desert regions. In stark contrast to the

---

1. James M. Monson, *The Land Between* (Highland Park, Ill.; Jerusalem, Israel: Institute of Holy Land Studies, 1983), p. 14.

well-watered plains along the sea, the Palestine wilderness is one of the most barren and desolate regions in the world. Life in this dry, hot, lonely, and dangerous region is often reduced to mere survival.

Yet, the desert plays a very important role in Scripture. These desolate wilderness areas taught some of the greatest heroes of faith to walk with the Lord. Moses spent two thirds of his life in the desert. David spent his youth and most of his early adulthood there. John the Baptizer began his ministry in the desert. Jesus faced Satan's temptation in the wilderness. Paul spent his first years as a Christian there. Clearly, the wilderness taught them to depend completely on the Lord.

The Bible emphasizes the role of the desert in spiritual formation, and this encourages us to attach value and significance to our suffering. We may not be in a physical, barren wilderness, but we must deal with the harsh realities of our trials. Our response to pain improves as we reflect on those who, like David, developed a passion for God "in a dry and weary land where there is no water" (Ps. 63:1). Just as the land of Palestine shaped the Israelites into a people dependent on the Lord, our Father longs to shape us during our desert times.

As you read your Bible, pay attention to the lay of the land. Keep a map handy as you study. You'll discover the key role that the topography of the land plays in the story of redemption.

Bibliography

Monson, James M. *The Land Between: A Regional Study Guide to the Land of the Bible.* Highland Park, Ill.: Jerusalem, Israel: Institute of Holy Land Studies, 1983.

Rasmussen, Carl G. *The Zondervan NIV Atlas of the Bible.* Grand Rapids, Mich.: Zondervan Publishing House, Academic and Professional Books, 1989.

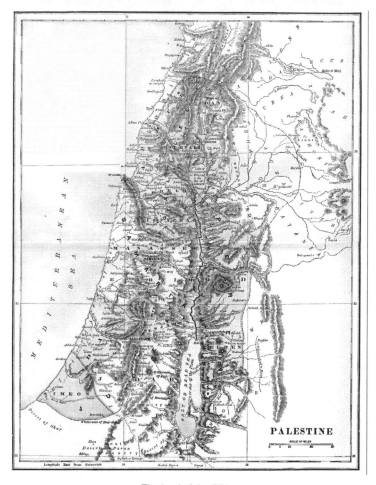

The land of the Bible

SECTION 2

DISCOVER
IT FOR
YOURSELF

THE IMPORTANCE OF UNDERSTANDING SCRIPTURE'S CONTEXT

by Jason Shepherd

Greet one another with a holy kiss."

Does anything about that command bother you or at least make you feel uneasy? It seems a little odd, but hey, it's a command from the Bible so we ought to obey it, right?

Before you greet your pastor with a wet sloppy kiss next Sunday, study the verse a little closer. Particularly, look at the cultural context in which Paul gave the command. With a little study, you'll discover that a kiss in Paul's day was quite different from a kiss today. It often communicated respect and honor rather than romance or affection. So Paul, by commanding Christians to kiss, was telling them to show respect and honor toward one another, not to display affection.

Because kissing has a different meaning in most modern cultures and would be inappropriate for Christians to practice today, does that mean the command, and perhaps other passages in Scripture, don't apply anymore? Absolutely not. Although the *practice* of a holy kiss is no longer relevant, the *principle* of showing respect and honor is still applicable.

The fact remains, however, that many passages—including this one—can be easily misapplied if we fail to understand the context in which they were written. Only by determining the historical contexts of the books of the Bible can we ensure that we're interpreting and applying them the way they were intended to be.

How to Discover the Biblical Context

How, then, can we learn to determine the historical context of a given book of the Bible? The first thing we need to do is ask questions. Don't be afraid to interrogate the text. Every time you study a passage, you should sit it down in front of you, shine a bright light in its eyes, and start drinking stale, day-old coffee. Then, in the gruff voice of an overworked cop, ask it:

✔ When were you written?

✔ Who was your author? In what time, place, and culture did he grow up and live?

✔ For whom were you written? In what time, place, and culture did your audience live?

✔ Why were you written? What was the occasion and purpose? (For example, were you written to warn? To refute heresy? To encourage?)

✔ In what genre do you fit? Are you a history, work of wisdom, letter, or prophecy?

Aside from the tough cop routine, which is just for fun, you can learn a lot by asking these questions. They can help you identify the pertinent details that unlock the book's meaning.

Knowing the *author*, for example, can have a significant impact on our understanding of a book. Take the letter of 1 Peter, which states, "To sum up, all of you be harmonious, sympathetic, brotherly, kindhearted, and humble in spirit" (3:8). Wait a minute! Are we to believe that *Peter* was the one who penned these words? The Peter who wanted to stop forgiving after the seventh offense; the Peter who refused to have his feet washed; the Peter who sliced off the guard's ear in the Garden of Gethsemane?

It's hard to believe that this Peter, with his fiery personality, would place gentleness and love so prominently in his correspondence. Then again, doesn't this fact make his instructions all the more meaningful? It does! If Peter, who was so disinclined to these concepts, came to realize how important they were, all the more important for us to do the same.

Identifying the *purpose* of a biblical book can also be important. A recently published work, an exposition of 1 John, had an interesting premise. The author, believing that the Christian community is filled with people who think they're saved but really aren't, presented a handful of "vital signs" from John's letter and challenged his readers to examine themselves, to take their spiritual pulse, and to make absolutely sure that their faith is alive enough to get them into heaven.

Unfortunately, the author of this book failed to understand (or flat-out ignored) John's reason for writing his first letter. The apostle's purpose, in fact, was quite the opposite. John did not write to people who thought they were saved but weren't. Rather, he wrote to people who thought they were *not* saved, but *were*. The "vital signs" contained in the letter were meant to comfort, not challenge. Oh that the author, or the editor, or the publisher would have taken the time to understand John's purpose!

Finally, we should never ignore the *genre* of a book. How many times have you heard someone claim a "promise" from the book of Proverbs? Here's a good one: "Do not be wise in your own eyes; Fear the Lord and turn away from evil. It will be healing to your body And refreshment to your bones" (Prov. 3:7–8). Sounds good, doesn't it? In fact, it sounds like a promise—if you fear God and abstain from evil, then He'll heal and refresh your body.

Problem is, hundreds of examples exist in Scripture in which someone did this very thing and received the exact opposite from God, Job being the most glaring example. He was the most righteous man of his time (Job 1:1), and yet God allowed him to be struck down with the worst demonic oppression in recorded history.

In the case of Job, did God break His promise in Proverbs 3:7–8? No. The problem is not with God going back on His Word; it's with our misunderstanding of His Word. The book of Proverbs does not give promises, it presents normative truths—principles or guidelines that are normally true, but not always. So Proverbs 3:7–8, when properly understood, teaches us that people who live righteously normally live in peace and health. But there are exceptions. When those exceptions happen, God is not breaking a promise. Rather, life is progressing naturally. Only by knowing the nature of the Proverbs can we avoid falsely accusing God, and only by understanding the genre of a book can we interpret it properly.

These details—author, purpose, and genre, as well as others—can affect the meaning of the various biblical texts and how we are to apply them. Asking the right questions is the key to finding the right interpretation and application of any given passage.

So, before you get yourself into trouble by kissing unsuspecting pastors, take note of the context of the verses you're reading. At best, the context will help you stay true to the Scriptures, and at the very least, it will save you some embarrassment.

EIGHT WORDS YOU NEED TO KNOW ABOUT YOUR RELATIONSHIP WITH GOD

by Taylor Gardner

If theological concepts and words puzzle you in their complexity, you'll love this accessible look at eight of the most important concepts in the Christian life.

On each of the following pages, get a word-at-a-glance explanation, suggestions to apply this concept to your day, key Scriptures about this concept, and suggested tools to go deeper in its description. You may even want to study one topic a day for your own Bible study. Get ready to explore these key words:

GRACE	**REPENTANCE**
FORGIVENESS	**ASSURANCE**
FAITH	**PRAYER**
DISCIPLINE	**HOLINESS**

GRACE

What does it mean to "wake up to grace?" What is grace? Answer: It's that part of God's character which shows us mercy by forgiving our sins! When we lie, steal, covet, gossip, or act immorally—we sin. God gives us grace by offering us forgiveness as a free gift. Does that seem surprising? We cannot earn His forgiveness; we can only receive it as a gift.

"*Nothing's* really free! Surely you have to do *something* to earn God's forgiveness." Not so! The Bible declares our salvation to be God's free gift. *Free* gift? Yes, pure grace! Nothing earned, nothing deserved. Bottom line, by making salvation available purely on the basis of grace, anyone can be saved.

Hard to believe? In grace, He forgives our sins, takes away our guilt, and promises us a home in heaven (John 14:2–3)! That's why God says, "Wake up and enjoy My grace!"

GRACE: Undeserved favor freely lavished on us by God when we accept His gift of Christ's death on the cross as payment for our sins. By His grace, we can live forever (John 3:16–17) and are released from the load of guilt (Matt. 11:28–30).

How the Bible Describes Grace

- Jesus Christ left the privileges of His throne in heaven and came to live and suffer in real poverty so that we could enjoy the riches of heaven (2 Cor. 8:9).

- God exercises His grace on our behalf, not because of what we've done or not done, but on the basis of what Christ did for us. In fact, He is more generous with His grace than we can believe (Eph. 1:7–8).

- We can come to God in any time of need and find Him gracious (Heb. 4:16).

Read more about grace: *The Grace Awakening* by Charles R. Swindoll (Word Publishing) and *What's So Amazing About Grace* by Philip Yancey (Zondervan Publishing Co.).

44

REPENTANCE

When Jesus said we have to repent (Mark 1:15) to be His followers, He was not saying 'have regret' or 'feel bad,' despite how the word is used today. Far from it. The word *repentance* is not about heavy shoulders or guilty consciences or shame. No. Those feelings arise when we need to repent. Repentance brings relief from them and opens the door for an active and hopeful way of life!

Repent literally means 'to stop, turn around, and head in the other direction.' We are to stop right where we are, admit we're going the wrong way, and believe there is a better way. This also means we need to turn from the path controlled by sin and self (whatever holds control over our lives), and walk straight into the open arms of our Father who knows us, understands and forgives us. We must not worry about the paths we've traveled before—the Father has never turned anyone away. Repentance replaces grief and guilt with comfort and joy!

REPENT: The decision to turn from wrong actions, attitudes, or words to those approved by God (Acts 26:20), to live in accordance with the decision to repent (Acts 26:20; Luke 3:8).

How the Bible Describes Repentance

- With great kindness and patience, God seeks to bring us to the place where we change our minds about sin (Rom. 2:4).

- Sometimes disobeying God's instructions causes us to experience sorrow and sadness, which help us change our minds and begin obeying Him. Deciding to obey is *always* the right choice (2 Cor. 7:10).

- God has a great longing in His heart for us to change our minds about sin and to turn to Him (2 Pet. 3:9).

Read more about repentance: *Restoring the Fallen: A Team Approach to Caring, Confronting, and Reconciling* by Earl and Sandra Wilson (InterVarsity Press) and *Inside Out* by Larry Crabb (NavPress).

FORGIVENESS

I don't know how God could forgive me for that.

I thought I forgave them, but found myself churning over it again the other day.

Sound familiar? Every Christian battles these emotions at one time or another. We can be guaranteed of forgiveness, however, when we find out what godly forgiveness is all about.

When God forgives us of a sin, He will never again bring it up. Sure, because He knows everything, He may remember that sin, but He chooses never to hold it against us. If we agree with Him about our sin, He forgives it. Thankfully, He keeps His promises, so we can be sure we're forgiven even when we don't *feel* forgiven.

How could His example change the way we forgive others? When we choose never to let others' past sins against us stand in the way of our present relationships, we follow God's example. This refreshing, forgiving attitude releases us from a bitter spirit and frees up others from their sins. We model God's mercy and grace every time we sincerely say, "You're forgiven."

FORGIVENESS:
to grant relief from payment (Acts 10:43; 13:38; Eph. 1:7), to give up resentment of or claim to requital (Eph. 4:32).

How the Bible Describes Forgiveness

- Jesus said there is no limit to how often we are to forgive each other (Matt. 18:21–22).

- *Confess* means 'to say the same thing.' God promises us that if we say the same things about our sins that He does, He *will* forgive us of our sins (1 John 1:9).

- God demonstrates how we can forgive others even as He forgives us (Eph. 4:32).

Read more about forgiveness: *The New Freedom of Forgiveness* by David Augsburger (Moody Press) and *Forgive and Forget: Healing the Hurts We Don't Deserve* by Lewis Smedes (Harper and Row, Publishers).

ASSURANCE

Satan loves to destroy our enjoyment of the Christian life by causing us to doubt our salvation. Peace quickly fades unless we're convinced of the security we have in Christ. Doubt also pressures us to *do* things to *look* spiritual rather than to focus on *becoming* spiritually mature. We can be sure His salvation begins the moment we receive His offer, and it lasts forever.

Assurance becomes ours when we realize acceptance of God's gift of salvation guarantees that nothing can separate us from Him. God did not allow our salvation to depend on us because we cannot become perfect by our own efforts. By allowing Jesus to pay the penalty of our sins, He could guarantee our salvation would never fail.

We won't gain assurance by what we do or don't do, but by what Christ has done for us (Titus 3:5; Eph. 2:8). Since our righteousness comes from Christ's work rather than our own, we gain peace through Him.

God *longs* for us to enjoy our security in Jesus Christ and the freedom it gives us to serve Him. With such blessed assurance, we serve Him out of love and gratitude. And that provides us with a little foretaste of heaven.

ASSURANCE: the state of being sure or certain (Rom. 8:38–39), having and accepting the knowledge of what God's grace provides for believers (Rom. 10:17).

How the Bible Describes Assurance

- God demonstrated His unconditional love for us through Christ before we knew Him (Rom. 5:8).

- God's Word was given to us so we can be assured of His love (1 John 5:13).

Read more about faith: *So Great Salvation: What It Means to Believe in Jesus Christ* by Charles Ryrie (Scripture Press Publications) and *Confident in Christ* by Bob Wilkin (Grace Evangelical Society).

FAITH

Faith is foundational to Christian living! Faith in what? Or whom? Ah, that's the rub. Many people have faith in their abilities, or possessions, or even in being born in America. Others have faith in having been born into a Christian family. Some just have faith in faith.

Until we start trusting God for salvation and for Christian living, faith impacts our lives very little. With Him as our foundation (1 Cor. 13:11), we can trust what God tells us in the Bible about how to live the Christian life.

Faith in Him gives meaning to our lives, and peace and contentment. Sure, trials are still a part of life, but we no longer face them alone. He is our friend, a true friend we can trust. No doubt we have come to the aid of a friend at one time or another and were so glad that we could. Likewise, He longs for us to bring our burdens to Him, and to ask for His help.

To summarize, we are saved by God's grace through faith (believing in Him). Placing our trust in Him enables us to serve Him with joy. Otherwise, it is impossible to please Him (Heb. 11:6).

FAITH: the unqualified acceptance of and dependence on the completed work of Jesus Christ to secure God's mercy toward believers (Rom. 1:17; 3:28), a gift of God (Eph. 2:8).

How the Bible Describes Faith

- True faith includes: *knowledge* of Christ's payment for our sins; *assent*, meaning we are convinced of this truth; and *volition* meaning we choose to trust Him (Rom. 1:17; 3:22, 30).

- To put it simply, faith gives us hope and conviction about things we don't see (Heb. 11:1).

Read more about faith: *The Facts of Faith* by Charles Edward Smith (Sherman, French and Company) and *In the Arena of Faith: A Call to a Consecrated Life* by Erich Sauer (William B. Eerdman Publishing Co.).

PRAYER

Sooner or later, everybody prays. It may be only a last-ditch stand against some disaster or death, but everybody prays. Many people say prayers. That is, they read or quote a prayer someone has written in the hopes it will help them stay on God's good side. But is that about all there is to prayer? Not really. Praying is talking to God about everyday life, like we would talk to a friend who really loves us.

We may be tempted to think that God listens to some people more than others—that someone else may have more clout with God. Think again! It really comes down to this: He loves for us to take time to talk to Him, tell Him our joys, our burdens, our desires, our needs, and so on. And guess what? When we talk to Him about these things, we're praying. Don't complicate it by trying to use unnecessary theological jargon. Just talk to Him.

How the Bible Describes Prayer

PRAYER:
Talking to God (Luke 23:39–43). To pray is to speak audibly, in song, writing, or thought.

- Jesus frequently spent much time talking things over with His Father. Enjoy the benefits of following His example (Luke 6:12).

- A serious conversation with God can be very tiring, but it brings great benefit (Luke 23:42–43).

- God desires for us to talk to Him in behalf of others (Acts 12:5; Eph. 6:18–20).

- Talking to God brings peace to our lives (Phil. 4:6–7).

Read more about prayer: *Bible Men of Prayer* by E.M. Bounds (Zondervan Publishing House) and *Sense and Nonsense about Prayer* by Lehman Strauss (Moody Press).

DISCIPLINE

Ever thought of using *joy* in the same sentence with *discipline?* Most people associate discipline with pain, not joy. However, once we understand how completely God loves us, then we understand that He desires the things which are best for us. His goal always brings us the most joy and satisfaction in our lives. He lovingly focuses on helping and encouraging us, not on punishing us. Recognizing these truths brings joy to our hearts.

God uses discipline to minister to us according to our needs. When necessary, He uses it to bring us out of sin or to correct our wrong choices. And, yes, it can be painful. But we are encouraged when we realize He loves us too much to let us continue in sin.

Since Jesus never sinned, His discipline was for growth through instruction, training, and experience. It brings us joy when we recognize our understanding has been increased and our faith has been strengthened.

God will bring corrective discipline into our lives whenever necessary, but His real joy comes in helping us grow strong in faith and in our commitment to Him.

> **DISCIPLINE:**
> to instruct, to train, to correct (Prov. 12:1; 23:12), to cause to grow emotionally or spiritually (1 Tim. 4:7–8).

How the Bible Describes Discipline

- The happiest Christians are those who are submitting to God's discipline in their lives (Job 5:17–18).
- As we gain wisdom, we appreciate God's use of discipline (Prov. 12:1).
- Good discipline leads to godliness (1 Tim. 4:7–8).

Read more about discipline: *Disciplines of a Godly Man* by Kent R. Hughes (Crossway Books) and *The Discipline of Grace: God's Role and Our Role in the Pursuit of Holiness* by Jerry Bridges (NavPress).

HOLINESS

The mention of the word *holy* conjures up images of straight-faced, joyless people living in a narrow world with lots of rules.

Real holiness means something else altogether. When God saved us from our sin, He set us apart as His children. He pulled us out of the crowd to represent Him to the world. Holiness and godliness mean the same thing—becoming more like Christ.

Sanctification, which comes from the same word as holiness, can be defined as the gradual growth we experience as we surrender to God's Spirit, inviting Him to shape how we think, what we do, and what we want.

Holiness not only occurs the moment we invite Jesus Christ to be Lord of our lives, but it continues as our lives reflect His leadership. Think of it—we carry God around in our bodies! Living a holy life means making Him feel at home.

How the Bible Describes Holiness

HOLINESS: Separation to God (1 Cor. 1:30; 2 Thess. 2:13), the resultant state, the conduct befitting those so separated.

- After He created the world, God set apart the seventh day as the one which He rested (Gen. 1:3).

- God chose Israel, distinct from all other nations, for a specific relationship with Himself (Exod. 19:3–6, Deut. 7:6).

- God's character and actions set Him apart from everything else, making Him worthy of everyone's worship (Ps. 99).

- The Christian's life, set apart from others, is an example of God's character (Ps. 4:3; Rom. 12:1–2).

Read more about holiness: *The Knowledge of the Holy* by A.W. Tozer (Harper & Row, Publishers) and *The Pursuit of Holiness* and *The Practice of Godliness* by Jerry Bridges (NavPress).

BIBLE STUDY BY THE YARD

≡∥≡∥≡∥≡∥≡∥≡∥≡∥

by Jason Shepherd

A baby blanket requires one yard of material. A dress takes two. And a quilt? Well, let's just say you'd better stuff your wallet before you go to Fabric World. As with most hobbies, sewing requires that you know how much material to buy *before* you sit down at your machine to make something. Otherwise, you may find yourself with a half-made garment, making a mad dash back to the store before it closes.

Bible study, like sewing, requires materials. To do it well, you need an assortment of well-chosen books to draw upon before you sit down at your desk to examine any given passage. How many yards of books, though, do you need? If you look at the library of Mrs. Johnson, the seasoned Christian who has been reading the Bible for fifty years, you might conclude that you need a yard or two. If you inspect your pastor's office, however, you'll find that it can take ten or twenty yards. Visit a seminary professor, and you'll begin to wonder if it takes a football field's worth.

Before you go into "sticker shock" over the need to spend money on a Bible study library, just remember one thing—as Christians, our faith is the most precious thing we possess, and the Bible is our primary source of guidance, hope, and encouragement. Because we depend so much on the Scriptures, how can we afford not to devote some of our shelf space to the study of God's Word? We simply can't. We can, however, fill that space with some excellent books for a surprisingly small price tag. With the help of these works and a learning spirit, we can become able students of the Bible. With this in mind, let's take a quick look at some the books we'll need.

Books for Your Shelf

Most people can get their questions answered by only a yard or two of books. The key is not so much the number you buy, but the quality and kind. Below you'll find a categorized treatment of the best books to acquire first. As your library grows, you can buy more specialized works, but for now it's best to start collecting the basics. You'll want to acquire one selection from each category before buying a second book in any.

A Good Study Bible: The Ultimate Four-in-One Machine

Sometimes we can use so many study aids that we end up ignoring the Bible itself. That's why the first and most important acquisition for a Bible study library is a good study Bible. Study Bibles not only offer the text itself, but they include a wide variety of helps such as maps, a basic concordance, charts, articles, commentary notes, word studies, book introductions, and much more. The right choice is the Bible that best fits your personal study needs. Here are a few to consider: *The Nelson Study Bible* (Thomas Nelson Publishers), *The NIV Study Bible* (Zondervan Publishing House), *Life Application Bible* (Tyndale House Publishers), *The Believer's Study Bible* (Thomas Nelson Publishers), and *The Ryrie Study Bible* (Moody Press).

The right choice for you will feature the translation you prefer (NIV, NASB, NRSV, and so on), contributions from scholars you trust, and the types of helps you prefer. The only way to make a fully informed decision is to visit your local Christian bookstore and look through their samples.

A One- or Two-Volume Bible Commentary: The One-Stop Information Shop

Reading commentaries is essential to accurately interpreting the Bible. Even the most brilliant scholars use them. Many commentaries have been written for every book of the Bible, but it's best to start with a reliable one- or two-volume work. *The Bible Knowledge Commentary,* a two-volume set, features comments from members of the faculty at Dallas Theological Seminary (Victor Books). *The Evangelical Commentary on the Bible* (Baker Book House), edited by Roger Elwell, features comments from noted evangelical scholars in a single volume.

When you become ready to buy more specialized commentaries, look for ones that cater to your particular study style. One word of caution—exegetical commentaries make extensive use of Greek and Hebrew, and take more effort to understand. So if you choose to use an exegetical commentary, be prepared to work a little to get the information you seek. No matter what your preferences, though, a commentary survey such as *New Testament Commentary Survey* by D. A. Carson (Baker Book House) can help you make informed selections.

A Topical Treatment of the Bible: Biblical Theme-Trackers

If you've ever found yourself wondering what the Bible says about a specific topic, there are two topically oriented tools that can help you. The *Thompson Chain-Reference Bible* (Zondervan Publishing House) uses an extensive system of cross-references to help you find all the passages that pertain to specific topics. The *Topical Analysis of the Bible* (Baker Book House) provides the same kind of information, but organizes it differently, listing Scriptures according to category.

A Concordance: Find Out What the Words Mean

Have you ever wanted to know where your favorite preacher gets his insights when he says, "The history behind this word is . . ." or

"The root of this word means . . ."? Observations like these can often unlock the meaning of a verse or make it much more significant to us. The place to find this information is in a concordance. A concordance shows you the original Greek or Hebrew word behind the English translation and gives a short definition of the term. The most important factor in choosing a concordance is the translation—make sure it's the same as your Bible. Otherwise, you won't be able to find many of the words. The following is a list of concordances based on the most common translations: *Strong's Exhaustive Concordance* (for the King James Version, Thomas Nelson Publishers), *The NIV Exhaustive Concordance* (Zondervan Publishing House), *New American Standard Exhaustive Concordance of the Bible* (Broadman and Holman Publishers), and *The NRSV Concordance* (Zondervan Publishing House).

A Bible Survey: Get a Bird's-Eye View of the Bible

A Bible survey book is a unique reference tool that can help you easily understand each book of the Bible, its historical context, and its place in Scripture as a whole. A foundational work in this field is *Talk Thru the Bible* by Bruce Wilkinson and Kenneth Boa (Thomas Nelson Publishers). Another trustworthy resource is *The Compact Survey of the Bible,* edited by John Balchin (Bethany House Publishers). Insight for Living offers a survey: a five-volume set of Bible study guides titled *God's Masterwork.*

A Bible Atlas: Get Your Bearings

Did you know that when God commanded Jonah to go to Nineveh, Jonah went in exactly the opposite direction? The Bible records that he went to Tarshish. On a map, you'll see that Nineveh was to the east of Jonah and Tarshish was to the west—way, way out west. Thanks to a Bible atlas, we learn that Jonah was not only disobeying the Lord's command, but that he was being as defiant as possible. In addition to maps, Bible atlases also contain fascinating articles on the history of Bible lands and cultures. Some excellent atlases are: *Baker's Bible Atlas* (Baker Book House), *New Bible Atlas* (InterVarsity Press), and *The Moody Atlas of Bible Lands* (Moody Press). Again, choosing the right one for you means taking a trip down to the Christian bookstore and paging through the samples.

A Bible Dictionary or Encyclopedia: More Background Information Than You'll Ever Need

In studying a book written thousands of years ago by authors who lived in lands thousands of miles away, in cultures vastly different from our own, we're bound to run into many terms and concepts that are foreign to us. The best resource to help us bridge this enormous gap is a Bible dictionary or encyclopedia. The most comprehensive offering is the four-volume *International Standard Bible Encyclopedia* (William B. Eerdmans Publishing Co.). For more brief entries, the *New Bible Dictionary* (InterVarsity Press) offers a fine collection in one volume.

A Survey of Bible Doctrine: Drawing Out the Theology of the Bible

With all the in-depth study of the Bible we do, sometimes it's hard to see the forest for the trees. That's why it's helpful to read a survey of Bible doctrine, which can remind us what the Bible teaches about various subjects. From a survey of doctrine, we can find out what the Bible says about angels and the future and many other subjects. Charles Ryrie, a respected theologian, has written an excellent book called *A Survey of Bible Doctrine* (Moody Press).

There you have it! The best works in each category of Bible study. Remember, it's best to acquire one from each category before buying a second in any. What's the most painless way to add volumes to your library? Put them on your birthday, Father's or Mother's Day, and Christmas wish lists!

PUTTING ON YOUR SPIRITUAL SPECS

by Bryce Klabunde

I'm stumped. I don't see anything in these verses that applies to my life.

Have you ever said this to yourself while reading the Bible? The problem is not interpretation—you understand what the verses mean. It's the application of the passage that has you scratching your head. What do these verses mean to me?

When the words on the page are blurry, it helps to wear spectacles. And when the application is blurry, it helps to put on your spiritual SPECS.

SPECS stands for a simple Bible study method created by pastor and teacher Ray E. Baughman. The letters of the acrostic represent questions to guide your thoughts while reading Scripture. As you meditate on a passage, ask yourself:

Are there any
> Sins to forsake?
> Promises to claim?
> Examples to follow?
> Commands to obey?
> Stumbling blocks or errors to avoid?[1]

---

1. Based on the SPECS model by Ray E. Baughman, *The Abundant Life* (Chicago, Ill.: Moody Press, 1987), p. 112.

These questions can open your eyes to the rich treasures of application in the verses. Let's take a closer look at each point.

Sins to Forsake

In some verses, the sins to forsake lie on the surface like pebbles on the beach, such as the sins in Paul's list of fleshly deeds in Galatians 5:19–21. In other passages, you have to dig down and pick out the sins in the attitudes, actions, and events that the author describes. For instance, the Israelites displayed a lack of faith when they refused to enter the Promised Land. The Pharisees revealed judgmental arrogance when they dragged the adulterous woman into the public square. And Peter demonstrated pride when he rebuked Jesus.

When you spot a sin in a passage, record it in your Bible study notebook and ask the Lord to reveal to you similar shortcomings in your life. Then, pause and confess that hurtful attitude or careless action to the Lord so you can receive His forgiveness.

Promises to Claim

The promises of Scripture give our faith a solid footing when the storms of doubt and fear threaten to sweep us away. What are some promises you can cling to?

✔ The promise of eternal life (John 3:16)

✔ The promise of forgiveness (1 John 1:9)

✔ The promise of a future home in heaven (John 14:1–3)

✔ The promise of God's abiding presence (Heb. 13:5)

The list could go on and on. Make a note of the promises you see, and soon you'll have a long list to recall when you need encouragement.

Examples to Follow

After washing the disciples' feet, Jesus said, "I have set you an example that you should do as I have done for you" (John 13:15). Our principal example for Christian living is Jesus. He is our Shepherd, leading us along His path of compassion, service, and love.

Besides Jesus, other models of godly living can be found in Scripture. Here is just a small sample of the lessons we can learn from God's people:

✔ Abraham—faith in God

✔ Job—endurance through trials

✔ Esther—courage in the face of adversity

✔ Ruth—submission to God's will

As you read the Bible, look for models like these. The saints of Scripture can be your best friends when searching for sources of application.

Commands to Obey

Christians often spend a lot of time seeking God's will. We read books, attend lectures, and ask wise people for counsel. Sometimes, in all our searching, we overlook the most obvious expression of God's will—His commands. God already has told us His will; we simply have to find His commands and obey them.

Of course, we must consider the purpose and setting of the commands before we apply them. Not every command in Scripture is given directly to us. For example, God told the Israelites to sacrifice animals to atone for their sins. Jesus' atonement for our sins nullifies this law. Yet that doesn't mean we toss it out. We still can obey the *principles* of confession and forgiveness that underlie this command. Obeying the principles behind the law is often the best way to apply commands not given directly to us.

Stumbling Blocks or Errors to Avoid

The Scriptures warn us about false teachers—people who seek to trip us with their deceptive messages. According to Jude, these spiritual charlatans "change the grace of our God into a license for immorality and deny Jesus Christ our only Sovereign and Lord" (Jude 4). Paul called them "savage wolves," who "distort the truth in order to draw away disciples" (Acts 20:29–30).

Watch for warnings like these in the verses that you read. Write down the errors of the false teachers and their scheming strategies so that you can spot their stumbling blocks and avoid them.

Using Your SPECS

How can you make SPECS a regular part of your quiet time routine?

Here's one idea. Down one side of a sheet of paper, write the five questions with plenty of space between each one. Then, as you read a passage of Scripture, fill in the blank space with brief notes based on what you see. At the bottom of the page, write the heading, "Action Steps." Pick one or two points from your notes, and write down how you plan to put those principles into action. On the next page, we provide an example of how to apply the SPECS method to Mark 6:45–52.

When the application of a verse is blurry, put on your SPECS! It's amazing how relevant God's Word can be.

Jesus Walks on the Water
Mark 6:45–52

Sins to Forsake	v. 52	A hardened heart that prevents us from seeing Jesus in the storms of life.
Promises to Claim	v. 51	Jesus' presence during our storms.
Examples to Follow	v. 48	Jesus' willingness to enter the storm to be with those in need.
Commands to Obey	v. 50	"Take courage!" "Don't be afraid."
Stumbling Blocks to Avoid	v. 49	The fear that hinders us from trusting God.

Action Steps

1. The criticism I receive at work feels like waves beating against the full of my ship. But I will take courage that Jesus is more powerful than my enemies.

2. I will also take comfort that Jesus is with me during this difficult time. I plan to start each day at work releasing my fears to God in prayer.

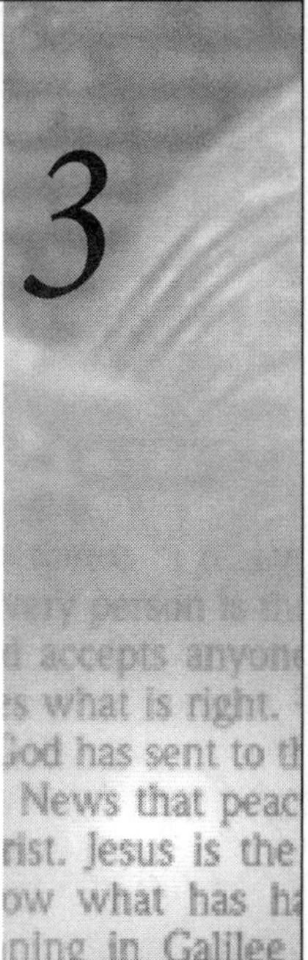

SECTION 3

SEE THE BIG PICTURE

THE BIBLE:
THE STORY OF THE AGES

by Barb Peil

"O ften, our knowledge of history is like a string of pearls without the string," an historian said. We have lots of isolated gems, but nothing to hold it together.

This seems especially true of Bible history. You may know individual stories in the Bible, but find it difficult to connect them in order. The following narrative traces the pearls of the Bible in chronological order, beginning with Genesis and ending with Revelation. As you understand how each gem fits into place, may you grasp more fully the riches of God's Word.

From Adam to Abraham,
> we have the history of the human race.

From Abraham to Christ,
> we have the history of the chosen race.

From Christ on,
> we have the history of the church.

Genesis   From the beginning, God, Who existed outside of time and place, desired a relationship with His creation. After creating a place for him to exist, God created Adam. Soon after, He created Eve for a companion. They enjoyed each other and God in a place perfectly suited for them and in a world of freedom and life.

However, this idyllic garden had one limitation: God said they should not eat the fruit from a certain tree, the Tree of Knowledge of Good and Evil. God's enemy, Satan, a former angel who rebelled under God's authority, stole the opportunity to enslave these creatures of God's affection and tempted them to distrust God's Word. Satan deceived Eve and Adam, who chose to disobey God. They both bore the painful consequence of separation from God. They were driven from the garden to protect them from eating of another tree, The Tree of Life. But even then, God wasn't finished with them. He now set in motion a plan to restore the intimacy with man that their sin had destroyed.

Life was hard for Adam and Eve. Their sons mirrored their parents' struggle with being distanced from God. Generation after generation grew more wicked, even though God had explained how to live correctly. Soon, God felt sorry that He had even created humanity and decided to wipe out the entire race. In His grace, He decided to spare the life of one man who was listening to God's Word. God told Noah to build a boat on which he and his family, as

68

well as two of each animal on earth, could live. Noah obeyed and when the world was covered by a torrent of water and everything living died, Noah and his family survived.

So God sent Noah, his family, and the animals off to repopulate the earth. It didn't take long before rebellion rose again. Men and women decided they would build a tower called *Babel* or 'gateway to God.' They wanted to approach God on their own terms. God touched their minds so they spoke different languages (that sounded like babble). In frustration, they disbanded to settle in different regions of the world.

It was time for God to lay the foundation for His plan to restore man to Himself. One starry night, He made a promise to a man named Abraham. God promised that He would make Abraham's descendants as many as the stars, and that He would give them, His people, a land for themselves and a blessing. When Abraham believed what God said, he instituted a pattern of faith for all of God's people to follow.

The next three generations, beginning with his son Isaac, followed by Jacob, and then Joseph, exemplified what it means to live by faith.

Job   There were plenty of dramatic twists and turns, but in the end, God proved faithful to His people.

Exodus through   Four hundred years after Joseph died,
Deuteronomy   God's people, Abraham's descendants (now numbering in the millions), were living as

69

slaves. God chose to rescue them from Egypt through His man, Moses. Understandably, the Pharaoh in Egypt didn't want to let his work force go or admit to a God greater than himself. So, he denied Moses' request to release God's people. After a dramatic and deadly contest of power, Pharaoh finally let them go. Soon into their journey back to the land that God had promised them, the people complained and doubted God. The consequence was forty years of wandering in an area that should have taken forty days to cross.

Joshua through 2 Chronicles, Psalms through Song of Solomon

After that generation had died, God raised up Joshua as Moses' successor to take the next generation into the Promised Land. After spectacular military campaigns where God made it obvious He was their leader, the children of Israel's faith was strong and God blessed them. But soon the predictable cycle began again. Since they had no king, a system of judges was established to keep the peace. But everyone did what they saw fit, regardless. They did, however, trust a godly prophet and priest named Samuel who had brought peace to their unruly land and had turned their hearts back to God. But the people weren't satisfied with how God directed them and pleaded for a king like every other country had.

So, after warning them of the consequences, God gave the people what they asked for: Saul as their king. But they soon grieved their choice. Though Saul was handsome and a great military leader, he lacked a heart for God. God soon anointed (this was a sign of His approval) Saul's successor, a shepherd boy named David. Insane with jealousy, Saul, for more than a decade, tried to kill David. But David's heart was fully surrendered to God, and God preserved His plan to bless His people through David. With David as king, God's people enjoyed a golden period of prosperity. Once the kingdom was passed on to David's son, Solomon, who had only a half-hearted devotion to God, civil war split the kingdom between his sons. Jeroboam and ten tribes made up northern Israel, and Rehoboam, with Israel's two other tribes, comprised Judah.

Isaiah through Zephaniah

For two centuries, Israel and Judah played a pyramid game with Syria. For several alternating generations of good and bad kings, God's prophets told His people to turn back to God or suffer the consequences of enemy capture. Sure to the prophets' predictions, the northern kingdom was captured by enemy nations and was never heard from again. The southern kingdom, Jerusalem, was destroyed and the nation was held in Babylon for seventy years.

Ezra, Nehemiah, Haggai, Zechariah, Malachi

Some of the captives were then allowed to return to rebuild Jerusalem, the temple, and the city walls.

In spite of the fact that they lived again in their land, God's people suffered from spiritual lukewarmness. They felt disappointed that God seemed to forget His promise, and they grieved the loss of their beautiful temple. And what's worse, God wasn't speaking anymore.

Matthew through John

The next time God's people heard from Him was four hundred years later when a voice crying in the wilderness commanded them to "make straight the way for the Lord." The voice, belonging to John the Baptizer, announced the hinge of history: the birth of the promised Messiah, the Lord Jesus Christ. God's plan to restore man's relationship to Himself now had a face and a name—*Jesus*, which means 'Yahweh saves.'

Jesus' early years passed without notice, except for a brief account in the temple when at the age of twelve, it became evident that His knowledge surpassed His years. Thirty years after the angelic announcement of His birth, Jesus went public with His identity and purpose. He came, taught, and discipled a small band of men, performed miracles, lived a sinless life, and gave up His life as a sacrifice for one express purpose: to seek and to save that which was lost. He submitted Himself to His Father's will and authority to restore the intimacy destroyed by sin so long ago in the garden. When Jesus rose from the dead, it was obvious that His sacrifice for man's sin had been accepted and a path now opened for all humanity to experience a restored relationship with God.

Acts

But God's plan was not complete. Forty days after Jesus resurrected from the dead, He ascended into heaven, His followers watching

Him rise into the clouds. His Ascension now allowed God to have a new relationship with man through His Spirit. Ten days later during the festival of Pentecost, God's Spirit filled every believing man, woman, and child. This event marked the beginning of the church, the living body of Christ.

The fervor of the early church caught on like wildfire. God used Jesus' disciples, especially Peter, to spread the word of salvation through Jesus Christ. The message was not only for God's people, the Jews, but for all the world. It was received with polar responses—people either embraced it or repelled it. Those that rejected the thought of Jesus as Messiah began to persecute these early Christians. Among the persecutors was a man from Tarsus named Saul. But God had other plans for him. He met Saul on a road through a blinding light, and confronted him with the truth of Jesus' identity. Saul responded in faith, changed his name to Paul, and after several years of study, began to proclaim Jesus as Savior throughout the world.

Romans through Jude Paul traveled the Mediterranean world establishing and ministering to churches in places like Corinth, Ephesus, Philippi, and even Rome. He wrote letters to them, as did other disciples, helping them understand God's desires for His people. Eventually Paul, like most of the apostles, gave up his own life for the sake of God's message.

Revelation

Only one disciple remained alive at the end of the first century: John, the beloved disciple. While living in exile on the island of Patmos, God showed him in a vision of what the final days on earth would be like, and how, once and for all, God would triumph over the evil that had invaded the Garden of Eden so long ago.

God's plan has always been to restore His people to an intimate relationship with Himself. He accomplished this through His Son, Jesus Christ, who came, lived among His people in a human body, and became the ultimate sacrifice for the sins of all humankind. One day, perhaps soon, Jesus will come again, as He specifically promised more than three times. As God's people wait for this incredible promise to become reality, God, in His grace, is waiting for all who would believe to come to Him.

If you haven't made that decision, why not do it today?

Bibliography

For a more thorough discussion of the Bible as a narrative, see these very helpful books:

Karen Lee-Thorp. *The Story of Stories.* Colorado Springs, Colo.: NavPress, 1995.

Henrietta C. Mears. *What the Bible Is All About.* Ventura, Calif.: Gospel Light Publications, Regal Books, 1999.

A TIMELINE OF HISTORY

by Barb Peil

Did you know that Daniel, Confucius, and Buddha all lived around the same time in history or that the Olympic games began in Jonah's day? Did you know that Cleopatra died just thirty years before Jesus was born?

By placing your favorite Bible passages in the context of history, you can discover even more intriguing historical facts.

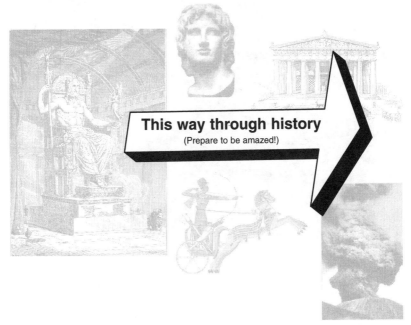

This way through history
(Prepare to be amazed!)

Undated – 2000 B.C.

Undated: Creation, the Flood, the Tower of Babel

c. 2500 B.C.: Great Pyramid at Giza built

Tower of Babel

2000-1900 B.C.

c. 2167 B.C.: Abraham is born

c. 2150 B.C.: The Babylonian king, Gudea of Lagash, engraves the earliest engineering graphics

c. 2066 B.C.: Isaac is born

c. 2006 B.C.: Jacob and Esau are born

c. 2000–1800 B.C.: Events in the life of Job

1800 B.C.

c. 1898 B.C.: Joseph sold into slavery

c. 1878 B.C.: Joseph restores his brothers, seven-year famine begins

c. 1876 B.C.: Jacob's family moves to Egypt (and stays 430 years)

Menhir

c. 1800 B.C.: More than 3,000 *menhirs*, or standing monoliths, are erected in several parallel rows at Carnac, France

1700 B.C.

c. 1790 B.C.: King Hammurabi of Babylon writes his *Code of Laws*

King Hammurabi

c. 1766 B.C.: The Shang Dynasty in China starts to make bronze

c. 1700 B.C.: Goldsmiths in Ireland and Wessex gain skill in forging gold into jewelry and warriors' ornaments

1600 B.C.

c. 1675 B.C. : Nomadic tribes introduce the horse-drawn war chariot into Egypt

c. 1600 B.C.: The Egyptians domesticate the cat, although they had worshipped it for more than 1,000 years

c. 1600 B.C.: Stonehenge, the megalithic monument in Wiltshire, England, reaches its final form

Egyptian Cat

Stonehenge

1500 B.C.

c. 1526 B.C.: Moses is born

c. 1525 B.C.: Pharaoh Thutmose I succeeds Amenhotep I in Egypt. Amenhotep I's tomb is the first to be located in the Valley of the Kings

79

1400 B.C.	1300 B.C.	1200 B.C.

c. 1446 B.C.: Israel's exodus out of Egypt. The wandering in the wilderness begins

c. 1445–1406 B.C.: Moses writes the Pentateuch

c. 1406 B.C.: Israel crosses the Jordan River into the promised land

c. 1390 B.C.: Joshua dies

c. 1380 B.C.: Period of the Judges begins (1375–1075 B.C.)

c. 1352 B.C.: Egyptian Pharaoh Tutankhamen dies

c. 1200 B.C.: The Iron Age begins in the ancient world

c. 1200–1020 B.C.: Setting of the book of Ruth (period of the Judges)

c. 1230 B.C.: Judge Deborah defeats Canaanite General Sisera in the Battle of Megiddo

1217 B.C.: Chinese astronomers record a solor eclipse for the first time

Eclipse

King Tutankhamen

80

1100 B.C.

1183 B.C.: Troy destroyed during the Trojan War

Trojan Horse

c. 1140 B.C.: Wen Wang creates the *Ling-Yo,* or Garden of Intelligence—the world's first zoo, covering 1,500 acres

1000 B.C.

c. 1075 B.C.: Samson fights the Philistines

c. 1050 B.C.: Saul is anointed as Israel's first king

c. 1010 B.C.: David becomes king

c. 1000 B.C.: The reindeer is domesticated in Siberia

c. 1000 B.C.: Oats are introduced into western Europe

c. 1000 B.C.: The first map of the world, depicting Babylon at its center, is written on a clay tablet

900 B.C.

Solomon's Temple

970 B.C.: Solomon's rule. He builds the first temple in 959 B.C.

c. 970–930 B.C.: Solomon writes many of the books of Proverbs, Ecclesiastes, and Song of Solomon

930 B.C.: Civil war divides the kingdom

800 B.C.

c. 875–848/848–797 B.C.: The prophets Elijah and Elisha minister

c. 800 B.C.: Greek epic poet Homer writes *The Iliad* and *The Odyssey*

c. 830 B.C.: The book of Joel is written

c. 800 B.C.: Underground aqueducts or *qanats* are built in Persia, which still provide much of the water in Iran today

c. 800 B.C.: The first sundials (still in use today) emerge in Egypt

700 B.C.

Olympic symbol

776 B.C.: The first Olympic Games are held in Greece

JUNE 15, 763 B.C.: Assyrians record a solar eclipse that is also recorded in Amos 8:9

c. 760–620 B.C.: The books of Amos, Hosea, Jonah, Isaiah, Micah, and Nahum are written

738 B.C.: Romulus, founder of Rome, invents a lunar calendar with ten months (winter is not counted)

722 B.C.: Assyria conquers Israel (ten tribes are never to be heard of again)

600 B.C.

609 B.C.: Daniel is taken captive

c. 620–600 B.C.: The books of Habakkuk and Zephaniah are written

c. 600 B.C.: The grape is introduced in France

c. 600 B.C.: King Nebuchadnezzar starts construction of the Hanging Gardens of Babylon, one of the Seven Wonders of the World

c. 600–570 B.C.: The books of Obadiah, Ezekiel, Lamentations, Jeremiah, 1 and 2 Kings, and Daniel are written

500 B.C.

586 B.C.: Babylon conquers Judah and takes its inhabitants into exile

563 B.C.: Siddhartha Gautama, founder of Buddhism, is born in India

551 B.C.: Confucius, Chinese philosopher, is born

c. 537 B.C.: Daniel is rescued from the lion's den

538 B.C. Israelites return to rebuild the land and the temple

c. 540–500 B.C.: The books of Zechariah and Haggai are written

Socrates

400 B.C.

c. 431 B.C.: The Statue of Zeus at Olympia, one of the Seven Wonders of the World, is sculpted

c. 464–435 B.C.: The book of Esther is written

465 B.C.: Persian king Xerxes (or Ahasuerus), Esther's husband, is murdered by his uncle, the head of his bodyguard

c. 460–430 B.C.: The books of Ezra, Malachi, 1 and 2 Chronicles, and Nehemiah are written

430 B.C.: Philosopher Socrates teaches in Greece

430 B.C.: The Old Testament closes and the four hundred silent years begin, with no direct revelation from God

300 B.C.

Plato

347 B.C.: Greek philosopher Plato, who founded the Academy, dies

c. 300 B.C.: The Pharos of Alexandria, one of the Seven Wonders of the World, is built. It is the model for lighthouses in the ancient world

323 B.C.: Military conqueror Alexander the Great, responsible for the spread of Greek language and culture, dies in Babylon

312 B.C.: Construction begins on the Appian Way—the ancient Roman road

200 B.C.

Halley's comet

240 B.C.: First recorded sighting of Halley's comet

Great Wall of China

225 B.C.: Construction begins on the Great Wall of China

c. 200 B.C.: The Romans invent concrete, used mainly for roads and seaports

100 B.C.

c. 100 B.C.: Glass windowpanes first used in Roman houses

Ice first used in China for refrigeration

Farming of the cocoa plant in South America

Farming of sugar cane in the Far East

Wind direction measured for the first time in Greece. Wind vane installed on the Acropolis

DECEMBER 12, 164 B.C.: Judas Maccabaeus regains control of Jerusalem, purifies and rededicates the temple, and restores Judaism (commemorated by the celebration of Hanukkah)

AUGUST 30, 30 B.C.: Mark Anthony, Roman triumvir, and his wife, Queen Cleopatra VII of Egypt, commit suicide in Alexandria, Egypt

37 B.C. Herod the Great begins to rule Judea

Cleopatra

0–A.D. 100

- c. 6–5 B.C.: Jesus is born

- c. A.D. 26: Jesus begins His ministry

- c. A.D. 30: Jesus is crucified, rises from the dead, and ascends into heaven

- c. A.D. 35: Paul's conversion

- A.D. 41–54: Emperor Claudius launches new chariot races in Rome by instituting animal fights after every five races

- A.D. 43–48: The book of James is written

- c. A.D. 46–48: Paul's first missionary journey

- A.D. 49: The Jerusalem Council meets and Paul begins his second missionary journey

- c. A.D. 48–51: The books of 1 and 2 Thessalonians and Galatians are written

- c. A.D. 50–69: The Gospel of Matthew is written

- A.D. 53–57: Paul's third missionary journey

- Late A.D. 50s: The books of 1 and 2 Corinthians and Romans are written

- Early A.D. 60s: The books Ephesians, Philippians, Colossians, 1 Timothy, Jude, and Philemon and the Gospels of Mark and Luke are written

- A.D. 64–65: The books of 2 Timothy, Hebrews, Titus, and 1 and 2 Peter are written

- July 18, A.D. 64: Half of Rome is destroyed by fire. Emperor Nero uses the fire as an excuse to persecute the Christians and begins an unpopular redevelopment plan for the imperial palace

- A.D. 67: Execution of Paul and imprisonment of Peter

- A.D. 70: The Romans destroy Jerusalem and burn the temple. The church and the Jewish people are scattered

- A.D. 73: The Romans destroy the ascetic community in Qumran. The Dead Sea Scrolls are kept hidden in nearby caves. The Romans attack the Jews hiding at Masada

- August 24, A.D. 79: Mount Vesuvius erupts, burying Pompeii and two other cities under ashes for centuries

- A.D. 90: John writes his Gospel and 1, 2, and 3 John

- A.D. 96: John writes Revelation

Bibliography

Biblical historical dates taken from "Old Testament Chronology" and "New Testament Chronology" charts, *The NIV Study Bible* (Grand Rapids, Mich.: Zondervan Publishing House, 1985) and "Old Testament Time Line" and "New Testament Time Line" in *The Nelson Study Bible* (Nashville, Tenn.: Thomas Nelson Publishers, 1997).

Biblical book dates adapted from "Divisions and Books of the Old Testament" and "Divisions and Books of the New Testament" in *The Nelson Study Bible* (Nashville, Tenn.: Thomas Nelson Publishers, 1997).

General historical dates taken from *The Encarta® 2000 New World Timeline* (Helicon Publishing Co, 1998) in *Microsoft Bookshelf* (Microsoft Corp., 1987–1999).

FASCINATING FACTS ABOUT THE BIBLE

by Barb Peil

The Word of God is an eternal, living book: God's direct communication with His people. It's also a historical book, written in history with all sorts of fascinating facts and information.

Did You Know?

- Egypt already had some pyramids when Joseph arrived!

- The Temple of Artemis (Diana) in Ephesus was one of the Seven Wonders of the World. It was built of white marble covered with gold and jewels.

- When Paul sent Titus to Croatia (Dalmatia, see 2 Tim. 4:10) he would have gone through Bosnia, Serbia, Yugoslavia, Albania, or Greece—if he traveled by land.

- The Great Wall of China was built and the Mayan Calendar was invented 200 years before Jesus was born.

- Paul never saw the Coliseum in Rome. The building project started four years after his death.

- Daniel, Confucius, and Buddha all lived in the same era.

- Jonah was sent to Nineveh, which is located in modern-day Iraq.

💡 When Daniel was taken captive and lived in Babylon the rest of his life, he lived in present-day Iraq.

💡 Queen Esther and the Greek philosopher Socrates lived in the same century. Esther's throne was in Susa, about one hundred miles from modern Kuwait City.

💡 King David predated the first Olympic games in Greece by about 200 years.

💡 Cleopatra died about thirty years before Jesus was born.

Test Your Knowledge of History

Q: What Old and New Testament site, considered to be one of history's oldest cities, has been literally destroyed and moved three separate times? (*Hint:* Joshua was responsible for one of its demolitions.)

A: *Jericho.*

Q: Near what modern-day country did the biblical sites of the Garden of Eden and the Tower of Babel most likely exist?

A: *Iraq, near the Tigris and Euphrates rivers.*

Q: What prolific non-biblical writer gives us a detailed history of Jewish and Roman life in the first century? (*Hint:* When he was captured and taken to Rome, he adopted a Latin derivation of his name, Joseph.)

A: *Flavius Josephus. Though original manuscripts are unavailable, copies of his books were preserved through the efforts of monks and early printing presses.*

Q: What desert summit, where a New Testament-era king built a palace, also sheltered an Old Testament king from a madman?

(*Hint:* It is also translated 'the stronghold.')

A: *Masada may have provided a safe lookout point for David when he ran from King Saul (see Ps. 27:1), as well as a three-year shelter from the Romans during the famous Jewish insurrection of A.D. 66–70.*

Q: The Apostle Paul most likely sailed past this Italian coastal city on his way to Rome. It was destroyed twenty years later by Mt. Vesuvius. What city was it? (*Hint:* This site became one of the most realistically preserved archaeological finds in history.)

A: *Pompeii, destroyed in its totality on the morning of August 24, A.D. 79.*

Bible-Related Facts You May Not Know

The Bible contains sixty-six books, written by forty authors, covering a period of approximately sixteen hundred years.

The word *Bible* comes from the Greek word *biblos,* meaning 'book.'

The word *testament* means covenant or agreement. God made an agreement based on law (Deut. 4:5), called the Old Testament, regarding man's salvation *before* Christ came. God's new agreement, or testament, was a covenant of grace (Gal. 3:17–25) and describes man's salvation *after* Christ came.

Jesus quoted from twenty-two Old Testament books.

The book of Hebrews quotes the Old Testament eighty-five times.

Revelation quotes the Old Testament 245 times.

The Longest, the Shortest, and the Most Unusual Verses in the Bible

Longest chapter: Psalm 119 (176 verses)

Shortest chapter: Psalm 117 (two verses)

Longest verse: Esther 8:9 (more than ninety words)

Shortest verse: John 11:35 (two words)

Longest book in the Old Testament: Psalms (150 chapters)

Longest book in the New Testament: Luke

Shortest book in the Old Testament: Obadiah (twenty-one verses)

Shortest book in the New Testament: 2 John (thirteen verses)

The oddest verse in the Bible: 1 Chronicles 26:18 (Look it up!)

Other than the word *the*, the word most often used in the Bible is *Lord*.

The two longest words in the Bible (it's a tie) read:

> *Jonath-elem-rechokim* (Ps. 56), means 'a silent dove of far-off lands.'

> *Maher-shalal-hash-baz* (Isa. 8:1), the name of Isaiah's son means 'quick to the plunder, swift to the spoil.'

In the King James Version, Ezra 7:21 contains all the letters of the alphabet except the letter *j*.

Prayer in the Bible

Shortest prayer in the Bible: "Lord, save me" (Matt. 14:30), when Peter was walking on the water and became afraid.

Longest prayers in the Bible: Nehemiah's prayer of praise and confession (Neh. 9:5–38) and Jesus' high priestly prayer (John 17).

THINGS WE CAN'T KNOW

The time of Jesus' return (Matt. 24:36).

How God's sovereignty works (Rom. 11: 33–36).

How the relationship between the Father, Son, and Holy Spirit works in the Trinity.

Who wrote the book of Hebrews.

The essence of eternity (Gen. 1:1; John 1:1).

God—unless we first know His Son, Jesus Christ (Matt. 11:27–29).

Some Extremes of the Bible

The Smallest Things Mentioned in the Bible:

A gnat (Matt. 23:24) An ant (Prov. 6:6)

A flea (1 Sam. 24:14) A mustard seed (Mark 4:31)

A *tittle*, part of a Hebrew language letter (Matt. 5:18 KJV)

The "Baldest" Men in the Bible:

Samson (Judg. 16:19) Elisha* (2 Kings 2:23)

Ezra (Ezra 9:3) Job (Job 1:20)

Paul (Acts 21: 23–24)

*The only naturally bald man recorded in the Bible.

The Hairiest Men in the Bible:

Esau (Gen. 27:11–23) King Nebuchadnezzar (Dan. 4:33)

Samson (Judg. 16:17) Absalom (2 Sam. 14:26)

Elijah (2 Kings 1:8) John the Baptist (Luke 1:15)

When the Sun Stood Still or Changed Directions

Joshua 10:12–13: It stood still as Israel fought against the Amorites.

2 Kings 20: 8–11: It changed directions as a sign to King Hezekiah.

Nine People Whom God Raised from the Dead

1. Elijah raised the son of the Zarephath widow (1 Kings 17:17–22)
2. Elisha raised the son of the Shunammite woman (2 Kings 4:32–35)
3. A man was raised from the dead when his body touched Elisha's bones (2 Kings 13:20–21)
4. Jesus raised the son of the widow of Nain (Luke 7:11–15)
5. Jesus raised the daughter of Jairus (Luke 8:41–55)
6. Jesus raised Lazarus after four days (John 11:1–44)
7. Many saints rose from the dead at Jesus' death (Matt. 27:50–53)
8. Peter raised Dorcas (Acts 9:36–41)
9. Paul raised Eutychus (Acts 20:9–10)

One Who Was Raised by Himself

Jesus rose from the dead (Matt. 28:5–9; Mark 16:6; Luke 24:5–6), and unlike any of the others listed above, He never died again.

Two Men Who Never Died

Enoch lived 365 years and then was taken up to be with God (Gen. 5:23–24; Heb. 11:5).

Elijah was carried by a whirlwind into heaven (2 Kings 2:11).

Seven Who Lived Almost a Millennium

1. Enos: 905 years (Gen. 5:11)
2. Kenan: 910 years (Gen. 5:14)
3. Seth: 912 years (Gen. 5:8)
4. Adam: 930 years (Gen. 5:5)
5. Noah: 950 years (Gen. 9:29)
6. Jared: 962 years (Gen. 5:20)
7. Methuselah: 969 years (Gen. 5: 27)

The Ten Most-Mentioned Women in the Bible

1. Sarah, Abraham's wife, fifty-six times
2. Rachel, Jacob's second wife, forty-seven times
3. Leah, Jacob's first wife, thirty-four times
4. Rebekah, Isaac's wife, thirty-one times
5. Jezebel, wicked queen and wife of Ahab, twenty-three times
6. Mary, Jesus' mother, nineteen times
7. Abigail, Nabal's and King David's wife, fifteen times
8. Miriam, Moses and Aaron's sister, fifteen times
9. Mary Magdalene, Jesus' friend, fourteen times
10. Hagar, Abraham's concubine, fourteen times

Eve, the mother of the human race, is mentioned only four times!

May these little-known facts not only bring a smile to your face, but also give you a greater love for the Book of the Ages—and the One whom it is all about.

THE BIBLE AT A GLANCE

=||=||=||=||=||=||=|||

by Barb Peil

Get a one-sentence overview of every book in the Bible.

Old Testament

The **Pentateuch** *means 'five books' in Greek and is the title of the first five books of the Bible, all of which are written by Moses and trace the history of the nation of Israel.*

- **Genesis** outlines the beginning of creation, man, and Israel, specifically chronicling the lives of Abraham, Isaac, Jacob, and Joseph.

- **Exodus** describes the "going out" of Israel from Egypt and their struggles to obey a holy God who wanted to "tabernacle," or dwell, with them.

- **Leviticus**, God's guidebook, offers the newly redeemed Israel the way to worship, serve, and gain access to God.

- **Numbers** transitions God's people from their wilderness wanderings to their place in a new land by illustrating divine consequences for rebellion.

- **Deuteronomy**, the second law, records Moses' swan song, stressing the importance of loving God and obeying Him with all your heart.

*The **Historical Books** trace key events in Israel's turbulent history from the time they conquered the land, through their spiritual and political downfall, and finally, to their return from exile.*

- **Joshua** chronicles the military campaign to reclaim Israel's land; however, they learn that victory is found through faith in God alone.

- **Judges** contrasts Israel's past obedience to the necessary consequences when everyone did what was right in their own eyes.

- **Ruth** tells the beautiful love story between King David's great-grandparents and affirms that God will provide for and protect His children.

- **1 and 2 Samuel** tell of the adventures and reigns of Israel's first two kings: Saul and David, the man after God's heart.

- **1 and 2 Kings** trace the political line of Israel, beginning with King Solomon, whose heart was divided, and end with a nation whose people were divided.

- **1 and 2 Chronicles** mirror the history of 1 and 2 Kings, yet concentrate on the spiritual lives of Judah's kings who modeled their hearts after David's.

- **Ezra** follows the exiled people's return back to the land as God promised and describes a new beginning for Israel.

- **Nehemiah** outlines the administrative genius and faith of a man who would rally God's people to rebuild the protective walls of Jerusalem in fifty-two days.

- **Esther**, set between the time of Ezra 6–7, tells the true Cinderella story of how God delivered His people from a holocaust-like plot.

Wisdom and Poetry Books delve into the very personal issues of walking with God, as well as explore real-life faith "under the sun."

✡ **Job** records the drama of a godly man who, after losing his health, wealth, family, and status, chose to trust that God was at work behind the scenes.

✡ **Psalms**, the hymnbook of the Bible, exalts God as worthy of all praise through songs that continue to be sung to this day.

✡ **Proverbs** teaches wisdom for living in short, pithy statements about everyday aspects of life and relationships.

✡ **Ecclesiastes** outlines Solomon's intense search for the meaning of life, ultimately finding it in knowing and loving God.

✡ **Song of Solomon** details the intimacies of marital love and metaphorically pictures the love of God for His people.

Prophetic Books foretold the consequences of Israel's refusal to live by God's Word in order to turn Israel back to God. They condemned man's sinfulness but also assured Israel of God's mercy.

Isaiah condemns Judah for their sin, and predicts God's judgment, but also offers comfort in God's faithful, future blessing.

Jeremiah describes Judah at the depth of spiritual decay and announces the heartbreaking news of God's judgment in light of His holiness.

Lamentations calls the people of Israel to mourn in this funeral liturgy for Jerusalem. Forty years later, Jeremiah's prophecy came true.

Ezekiel administers hope to exiles in Babylon that God's name would be honored and that His glory would not be forgotten.

- **Daniel** assures Israel and the world that God is sovereign and will work in the lives of individuals as well as in history, according to His own will.

- **Hosea** symbolizes God's faithfulness and the spiritual adultery of Israel by marrying and loving a prostitute.

- **Joel**'s "day of the Lord," describes Israel's present disaster and future tribulation, but also promises hope for those who believe.

- **Amos** foretells judgment coming to Israel in spite of the prosperity they now enjoy, and urges them to turn back to the Lord.

- **Obadiah** retells the ancient rivalry between Esau and Jacob in the new context of Edom warring—and losing—against Israel.

- **Jonah** emphasizes God's grace in giving wicked people an opportunity to respond to the Word and will of God. The prophet Jonah learns several lessons too.

- **Micah**'s message of judgment echoes in a sin-saturated society where justice is absent, but a Divine Deliverer will be coming soon.

- **Nahum**, meaning 'comfort,' offers encouragement to Israel that the Assyrians would not go unpunished for their wickedness.

- **Habbakuk** tells of the personal struggle the prophet felt with God's plan to judge Israel using a more wicked nation. Waiting and trusting God is Habbakuk's resolution.

- **Zephaniah** speaks of both the wrath and mercy of God for Israel and Gentile nations, for the present and the future.

- **Haggai** rouses enthusiasm for the rebuilding of the temple and calls people to renewed courage, holiness, and faith in God.

Zechariah challenges people to look ahead in God's plan and see the benefit of their work in rebuilding the temple.

Malachi urges Israel to be faithful in spite of their questions regarding God's love and protection of His people.

New Testament

As the fulfillment of the Old Testament, **The Gospels,** *along with the book of* **Acts,** *provide the historical and theological backdrop for the rest of the New Testament. Together, they provide a composite picture of the work and person of our Lord Jesus Christ.*

Matthew presents Jesus as the Christ, Israel's messianic King, and the fulfillment of Old Testament prophecy.

Mark pictures Jesus as the Suffering Servant, the Savior who came to give His life as a ransom for mankind.

Luke describes Jesus as the Son of Man, whose mission was to "seek and to save that which was lost" (19:10).

John presents Jesus as the eternal Son of God who offered eternal life to all who would believe in Him.

Acts paints the only historical portrait of the newly born church, from Jesus' ascension to Paul's missionary travels.

For the first time, God used personal letters as a vehicle for divine inspiration. These letters, most of which were written by the Apostle Paul, addressed specific problems and issues that had timeless and universal application.

Romans explains the significance of Jesus' death, clarifies what it takes to be accepted by God, and illustrates how to live a godly life.

☐ **1 Corinthians** addresses a variety of problems that faced the early church: moral and ethical, doctrinal and practical, and corporate and private.

☐ **2 Corinthians** rejoices that the church in Corinth experienced a change in heart and was now accepting Paul and each other in their God-given roles.

☐ **Galatians** urges believers to not give up their freedom in Christ in exchange for either loose living or legalism.

☐ **Ephesians** reminds believers of the great spiritual wealth that is theirs because of their inheritance in Christ.

☐ **Philippians** urges believers to focus their lives on the joy and encouragement found in Christ, regardless of their circumstances.

☐ **Colossians** affirms the supremacy of the person of Jesus Christ and the completeness of the salvation that He provides.

☐ **1 Thessalonians** calls believers to excel in their faith and love for one another and to always be thankful.

☐ **2 Thessalonians** comforts believers who are suffering and urges them to continue trusting God in light of future events.

☐ **1 Timothy** encourages leaders how to conduct themselves, guard against false doctrine, and develop mature leadership in the church.

☐ **2 Timothy**, Paul's final letter, pictures a very personal portrait of what it means to finish well and remain faithful to the very end.

☐ **Titus** offers practical wisdom for church organization and leadership, emphasizing good works as an evidence of faith.

☐ **Philemon** asks a slave owner to extend forgiveness to a runaway slave because of the grace extended to him in Christ.

📧 **Hebrews** appeals to Jewish believers, who because of great persecution, wanted to turn back to Judaism.

📧 **James** integrates true faith and everyday practical living by saying faith is visible in the way we choose to live our lives.

📧 **1 Peter** illustrates that persecution can cause you to grow or grumble, so choose whether hard times will create—or destroy—your character.

📧 **2 Peter** reminds believers of the timeless truths of the faith and encourages them to continue growing through spiritual maturity.

📧 **1 John** explores the relationship between God and His people in terms of light, love, and eternal life.

📧 **2 John** affirms that Christians should love each other, but warns that hospitality shouldn't be extended to those wanting to destroy the truth.

📧 **3 John** commends believers who are making their faith an active part of their lives and godly character their priority.

📧 **Jude** reveals the true nature of false teachers and encourages believers to fight for the faith.

☣ **Revelation** completes God's story, begun in Genesis, with a dramatic description of God's plan for the end of the world.

BEHIND

THE

SCENES

ABOUT THE AUTHORS

Charles R. Swindoll

The president of Dallas Theological Seminary and a best-selling author, Chuck also serves as pastor of Stonebriar Community Church in Frisco, Texas, where he's able to do what he loves most—teach the Bible to willing hearts. His focus of practical Bible application has been heard on the *Insight for Living* radio broadcast since 1979.

Larry Sittig

A graduate of Dallas Theological Seminary, Larry is a pastoral counselor with Insight for Living who daily helps others apply God's Word to difficult situations in their lives. His previous ministry experience includes service as a missionary to Spain.

Bryce Klabunde

A graduate of Dallas Theological Seminary, Bryce joined Insight for Living as a study guide writer in 1991. He now serves as director of pastoral ministries, responding to the needs of listeners with truth and hope.

Mike Balsbaugh

A graduate of Western Baptist College and Talbot School of Theology, Mike joined Insight for Living as a pastoral counselor in 1987. Daily, Mike meets listeners where they are and guides them in their relationships with the Heavenly Father.

Jason Shepherd

Jason joined Insight for Living as a study guide writer in 1998, helping to bring the truths of God's Word home to listeners. He is a graduate of Texas A&M University and Dallas Theological Seminary.

Taylor Gardner

A doctoral graduate of Dallas Seminary, Taylor has served in Insight for Living's pastoral ministries division for eleven years and as its director since 1996. Through counseling and discipleship, Taylor loves helping people realize God's great grace in the midst of their problems.

Barb Peil

With the heart of a teacher, Barb has contributed to Insight for Living as a staff writer since 1994. One of the first women to graduate from Dallas Theological Seminary, she is also an adjunct instructor at Biola University.

ADDITIONAL RESOURCES FROM INSIGHT FOR LIVING

How else can you help me grow in my understanding of the Christian life?

If you want to grow, Insight for Living wants to help you—whether you've recently trusted Christ as your Savior or have walked with Him for years. Our goal is to help you gain new insights into the Bible through a variety of resources:

✔ An encouraging **monthly letter from Chuck Swindoll**

✔ An instructional, thought-provoking **monthly newsletter**

✔ More than 100 different **Bible-teaching cassette series** to encourage you toward godly living. Subjects range from Bible book studies and Bible character portraits to topical surveys—all from Chuck's reliable, applicable, and enjoyable teaching ministry. (Request a cassette series listing for more information.)

✔ **Bible study guides** that correspond with every cassette series topic for your personal or group study.

✔ **Pastoral counseling by mail** for trustworthy spiritual answers about life's difficult questions

✔ **Christian books you can trust** for spiritual growth, character building, and doctrinal authenticity.

Call or write for more information about any of these resources.

We'd love to help you find the resources that best fit your needs. We're looking forward to hearing from you.

www.insight.org

United States
Insight for Living • Post Office Box 69000 • Anaheim, CA 92817-0900
Toll-free 1-800-772-8888, 24 hours a day, seven days a week

International locations, call (714) 575-5000,
8:00 A.M. to 4:30 P.M., Pacific time, Monday through Friday

Canada
Insight for Living Ministries • Post Office Box 2510
Vancouver, BC V6B 3W7
Toll-free 1-800-663-7639, 24 hours a day, seven days a week

Australia and the South Pacific
Insight for Living, Inc. • GPO Box 2823 EE
Melbourne, VIC 3001, Australia
Toll-free 1800-772-888 or (03) 9877-4277
8:30 A.M. to 5:00 P.M., Monday through Friday